33

$ 3.⁰⁰⁄₀₀

History

THE PEOPLE OF THE ANCIENT AMERICAS

THE
PEOPLE OF
THE ANCIENT
AMERICAS

COTTIE
BURLAND

PAUL HAMLYN
LONDON NEW YORK
SYDNEY TORONTO

To Egerton Sykes
Founder of the Journal
New World Antiquity
and proposer of the series of lectures
delivered by the author at Morley College
which were the basis of this book

Published by
The Hamlyn Publishing Group
London   New York   Sydney   Toronto
Hamlyn House
The Centre
Feltham
Middlesex

SBN 600 02813 5

Printed in Hong Kong by
Toppan Printing Company (H.K.) Limited

Contents

Introduction 8
The Beginning of the Americas 11
Northwest Coast Indians 21
The First Farmers 33
The Beginnings of Mexico 45
The Aztec Power 69
The Maya People 85
The Peoples Between 109
The Beginnings of Civilization in Peru 119
The Inca Power 143
Conclusion 155

Further Reading List
Acknowledgments
Index

Colour Plates

Indian woman of Florida, 1587 18
A warrior of the same race 18
'Totem Pole' rock, Monument Valley 19
Pueblo Indian house block 22–3
An Indian of the Plains 26
Navajo mother and her family 27
Monument Valley, Utah 30–31
Dakota painting on deerskin 31
Giant Olmec stone head 49
Monte Alban. The great plaza 49
Tajín. The ball court 52
Codex Vindobonensis Mexicanus I 52
Gold pendant from Monte Alban 53
Moctecuzoma's headdress 53
The Nebaj vase 56–7
Xochipilli 56
Palenque. The Temple of the Inscriptions 57
Labna. Ceremonial archway 60–61
Chich'en Itzá. The Temple of the Warriors 60
Chich'en Itzá. The plumed serpent 60
A potter of Guanajuato 64
Uxmal. The Temple of the Sorcerers 64
Bonampak. Fresco from the south wall 98
Palenque. The Temple of the Sun 99
Barefoot dignitary. Maya priest 102
Maya snail vase 102
Uxmal. A general view 103
Young man, Kashinaua tribe 106
Father and son, Waura tribe 106
Kraho tribesmen 107
Chimú goldwork 110
Stone head from Tiahuanaco 111
Tapestry, central coast of Peru 128
Paraccas textile fringe 128
Paraccas textile. Warriors 128
Lake Titicaca 132
The walls of Sacsahuaman 132
Macchu Picchu 133
Gold pectoral ornament, Ecuador 136
Gold pendants, Colombia 136
Quechua Indian, northern Peru 137
Chimú pottery figure 140
Recuay pottery vessel 140
Mochica portrait vases 140–141
Nasca vase 141
Mochica mythological vase 141
The Intihuatana 144

Introduction

This book arose from a series of lectures given to adult students at
Morley College and has the same basic purpose as those lectures:
to give a groundwork of knowledge about pre-Columbian America
which can later be amplified by further study. Such a book seems to us
to be very necessary at the present time because of the growing
interest in non-classical archaeology, and particularly in the
antiquities of the fascinating double continent of the Americas.

There are many fewer sources available for this sort of study than
there are for other areas of history. They consist of first-hand reports of
European observers of the final stages of American Indian autonomy
in the various areas of the continent. For Mexico and Peru there are
histories written down by native noblemen or dictated by tribal
elders after the period of the conquest. From Mexico itself the record
between about 650 A.D. and 1520 is given in a scanty series of painted
documents in the native ideographic system, the famous Mexican
codices. Otherwise all our information comes from modern archaeological studies. This work has magnificent aid from the results of
radio-carbon dating, which is reasonably accurate – within half a
century in the earliest period of nearly 20,000 years ago, and within a
decade in the sixteenth century. Where tribal names are used they are
ones known at the time of the first contact with Europeans.

From a mass of interesting data and a number of fine regional
studies we have been able to condense a kind of skeleton description
which we hope will prove of interest to the general reader and of use to
the specialist.

The book frequently mentions the religions and mythology of the
regions we discuss, but this is deliberately restricted because of the
much greater amount of such material available in the series of books
on mythology from the same publishers.

The heroes and heroines of the book are the simple folk who hunted
animals and later dug the ground to produce food for their families.
From their simple beginnings something grew which flowered later in
the magnificent barbaric civilizations of the Aztecs and the Incas.
They had so few contacts, through the centuries of their development,
with any othe people that we may fairly say that ancient American
culture stems purely from the American Indian.

Who were the American Indians? Mostly people whose ancestors
had infiltrated into the Americas from the ancient hunting grounds of

Siberia. They are by no means a unified race because they did not enter the New World in any large single migration. They came in small groups of a few families at a time, on and off for more than twenty thousand years. Most are of medium height and reddish brown complexion. All have straight black hair on their heads and only sparse body hair. Some of the later entrants were taller and more coppery in colour, though the Eskimo, with their short stature and fawn coloured skins were also latecomers. So we can classify the Americans as a unified race only in that they were all Mongoloid in general features. Their blood-groupings vary a good deal, and the physical characteristics of any given tribe are so variable that we may well say that their great diversity is another point of unity. These are the people whose diversity is also seen in their achievements, some remained in simple savagery, attuned to their environment, but others trod a longer path, to brilliant civilisations which astonished the Europeans. Something of that remarkable story is the content of our book.

COTTIE BURLAND
1969

The Beginning of the Americas

Hundreds of millions of years ago, long before mankind was on the earth, the Americas were two continental islands. The northern one, covering the area of Quebec, some eastern parts of Canada and the United States, still survives as a geologic area known as the Laurentian Shield. The southern one remains in the very ancient mountains of Eastern Brazil, which are also among the earliest rocks to remain on the surface of the earth. Many millions of years later a great convulsion of the earth, probably due to contraction during cooling, caused enormous crumplings of rock, thus originating the Alps in Europe and the Himalayas in India. On the American continent this great upheaval produced the longest chain of mountains on earth. They start in Alaska and proceed southwards as the Rocky Mountains through Canada and the United States, continue as the Cordillera through Mexico and the Central American Republics down to Panama where, as a range of low volcanic mountains, they connect with the highlands of Colombia and then proceed as the Andes all the way along the west coast of South America as far as Tierra del Fuego, where they plunge under the ocean before reappearing as part of the Antarctic continent. After this enormous mountain chain arose the natural forces of erosion washed down great quantities of sand, mud and gravel from the mountains and so formed comparatively flat areas only a little above sea level, such as the Pampas, the Gran Chaco of South America, and the vast swampy basin of the Amazon river. In the north the whole area of the plains from Hudson Bay down to the Mississippi was similarly formed, but in the northern continent further complications arose during the glacial period. The immense fields of ice which ploughed their way down from Greenland and Labrador reached to the south part of what is now the Great Lakes area. As they melted they deposited great quantities of sand and gravel to form terminal moraines which blocked up the natural drainage and produced the system of the Great Lakes, the St Lawrence and the Mackenzie basins. Thus, throughout millions of years, of tremendous upheaval and slow development, America was prepared for its human population.

Animals must have reached America at quite an early period; otherwise there would not have been enough time for the evolution of such remarkable creatures as the giant sloth in South America, or even the llama, which is a distant relation of the old world camel.

The great mountain ridge of the Americas is the longest continuous mountain range on earth. The mountains of Alaska and the soaring Andes are part of the same chain.

The Americas extend
through almost every lati-
tude, from the Arctic wastes
of the Mackenzie River delta
to the bleak archipelago at
the tip of South America. The
Beagle Channel is one of the
many waterways through the
numbers of islands.

Bison on the American
prairie. These American
buffalo once roamed in vast
herds on the western plains
and were the chief source of
food and clothing of the
Plains Indians, who took
what they needed and left
the herds to thrive. The
indiscriminate slaughter by
the white man led to the
virtual extinction of the
bison, which is now care-
fully preserved in small herds
such as this one in the Nio-
brara National Wildlife
Refuge in Nebraska.

12

The Beginning of the Americas

In ancient times America was inhabited by mastodon, mammoth and a species of wild horse, as well as several (now extinct) varieties of bison, some of which were much larger than any of the present species. This world of grassy plains and woodlands, abounding in large animals which were an excellent source of food, became the home of several primitive tribes of hunters.

It seems probable that there were humans in America at least 50,000 years ago. From this period we have several rather coarsely flaked stone implements, associated with fireplaces where wood was burnt, suggesting that the places were camping sites of hunting tribes. But the finds are so few that we cannot come to any definite conclusion about the type of people who made them or even the real extent of their culture. From the stone implements it looks as if they were very primitive indeed, but that is by no means certain since many people in history have made quite elaborate instruments from wood without using stone. So we remain uncertain about the nature of these earliest human cultures of the Americas.

In the last glacial period there appear to have been several entries into America by small tribes of hunters passing over what is now the Bering Straits. The straits were at that time dry land; a great quantity of the world's water was held in solid form in the ice caps of the glacial period, so sea levels everywhere were about a hundred feet lower than they are at present. Bands of hunters followed the animals down an ice-free corridor on the eastern side of the Rocky Mountains leading towards the great plains. We have no reason, however, to think that they knew of warmer, brighter hunting grounds to the south. They were certainly capable of protecting themselves from the intense cold of this ice-free corridor

An Eskimo container carved from a walrus tusk. Caribou stags grazing and preparing to fight. A hunter approaches and shoots one of the stags. Note the conventional foreshortening used for the grazing animals in the herd, it is unusual to find this in primitive graphic art. Mid-nineteenth century. James H. Hooper Collection.

The Beginning of the Americas

Eskimo Art of the period 1000-1200 A.D., the Punuk culture of Alaska, seen on a knife handle. The linear decoration was engraved by stone points, and the small circles made by a drill. The blade was probably made of slate.

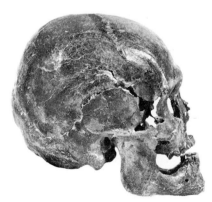

The skull of a Mexican man who died in a hunt 12,000 years ago. Called Tepexpan man, he was exactly the same physical type as his descendants of today.

14

by means of skin garments, so they could not have been completely primitive savages. They must have understood the ways of the animals and known a good deal about the most efficient methods of hunting, otherwise they would never have been tempted to pass through such a difficult land. Eventually we find them settled throughout the Americas.

More than 12,000 years ago there were people who made stone blades for spear and dart points in a cave in Tierra del Fuego, having traversed the whole length of the Americas. Still earlier, some 24-25,000 years ago, we find people established in the southern United States. They were hunting tribes with a highly developed flaked stone industry. They chipped flint and chalcedony with great precision, and probably used pressure-flaking points of bone just to knap off the tiny flakes necessary to make a very sharp edge to their tools. These stone points have been found not only in camp sites but also within skeletons of prehistoric bison and even great elephants.

It appears from some finds in the neighbourhood of Mexico City that some 12,000 years ago elephants had been chased into a swamp and were then speared by a band of hunters before they were able to extricate themselves from the mud. One of the hunters was killed and the skull, now preserved in the National Museum of Mexico, is that of a man who is practically indistinguishable in type from the American Indians of today. There is evidence that even at this early stage the populations of the Americas were racially mixed and probably had been when they entered the continent. The stature of the Mexican hunter whom we know as Tepexpan man was about five feet five or six inches. His people lived by their successful hunting of large animals; there is no evidence that they had knowledge of agriculture. Nothing suggests that any early men in the Americas ever built themselves more than a simple earth hut or perhaps a little skin tepee such as was used by the Plains Indians until the nineteenth century. One must assume that in early days the American Indian hunter was not dissimilar in culture from the prehistoric hunters of western Europe – the people who chased bison and mammoth over the plains of France and southern England. Unfortunately in America we have no cave art which can be ascribed to this period, but in Mexico there are two pieces of bone carved with animal heads which show that the primitive hunters of 12-20,000 years ago were by no means devoid of artistic talents.

It appears that climatic changes were the main cause of the early extinction of the large animals. The American horse, however, lasted until about 8,000 years ago, perhaps even a little later, and seems to have become extinct through human hunting. There were no horses left at any historic period in America until the Spaniards re-introduced them when they invaded Mexico.

In this immense continent of America with its grasslands, tropical forests and mountain plateaus, the Indians arrived as a very simple hunting people free to exploit whatever they found. In historic times the whole range of hunting cultures were still present; even as late as A.D. 1700 there were primitive Indians in California who lived mostly on wild roots and acorns, which they pounded into meal that was then leached out in warm water to take away the bitter flavour. They made this meal into a paste which they laid on stones heated over a fire.

The Beginning of the Americas

Thus they made thin white wafers of a very nourishing bread which they ate together with roots, vegetables, and small animals such as marmots, hares and even edible lizards. It was just possible for these simple hunters to live a satisfactory life. If more advanced tribes of Indians came their way they simply disappeared among the rocks and bushes. For them there had been no chance of acquiring a higher culture at any time because their territory was too barren. They achieved enough to live and had no reason to go further.

The development of the Eskimos was somewhat different. They also retained a Stone Age hunting system right into the nineteenth century, living in comparatively small communities. A group of Eskimos containing seventy individuals was a rarity, because it was difficult to get food for so many people by hunting. They lived in a country without vegetable food (though occasionally in summer a few berries were obtained) and nearly everything they had came from sea hunting. The products of their hunt produced all they needed for their life. They built snow shelters in winter and skin tents in summer. They used bones and walrus ivory for making tools. Sometimes they carved very beautiful things from ivory with stone blades. They had skins for making their clothing, and bone was used to make needles for sewing the clothing together. In other words the primitive Eskimo hunter could normally live a very comfortable life as long as there were not too many people in his tribal group. Sometimes, of course, climatic conditions became worse, the animals migrated at an unexpected season, or the ice melted too early, and then whole groups of Eskimos simply became extinct. If there was no food and no way of hunting it people died – and that was that. Their bones were found by people of later times who looked at them and wondered who they were, knowing that they were people of their own kind but with no history.

The natives of Tierra del Fuego lived in a more primitive state, right up to the nineteenth century. These people were the Yaghans, Alacaluf and Ona who lived by fishing and hunting around the Magellan Straits. They made small canoes from beech bark lashed to small boughs of trees. Their clothing was almost non-existent – the usual thing worn was a skin cape reaching only to the waist, and they changed it from one shoulder to another according to the direction of the wind. They made simple huts of boughs, sometimes covered with sods of earth but more often not, and they constantly needed to have small fires going in their huts. They also kept fires going on sods of earth which they put in their canoes. They were experts in collecting mussels and hunting sea-lions. Occasionally they were fortunate when a dead whale was washed up and could be cut to pieces, but they went in for very little marine hunting of the larger whales. Sometimes they hunted the guanaco – a small species of wild llama which provided them with their skin capes. Some of them learnt from the neighbouring Tehuelches of the pampas how to make larger skin robes which could be wrapped around one like a tent, and so keep off the cold winds which made the country such an unsympathetic place to live in.

There were tropical parts of the Americas in which people retained their palaeolithic way of life until the nineteenth century, and groups like the Botocudo Indians in the mountainous regions of Eastern Brazil who used exceedingly little stone. Their weapons were clubs and spears made of wood, the spear points were of barbed wood,

A ripple-flaked stone blade set in a short wooden shaft, from California, made shortly before 1900. This was made and used as a knife by one of the smaller and more primitive tribes who were yet masters of the art of stone flaking.

15

or occasionally of bone. The Botocudo wandered from place to place in small family groups within their hunting territories. They wore no clothing, having no need of such an invention in the humid tropical forests of their homeland. The heavy rain storms passed over them unheeded; they waded through the narrow rivers, climbed trees easily and made themselves fire with fire sticks. They had little need of any shelter, but occasionally they made wind-breaks of leaves. The basic furniture of the home was the hammock slung between trees, providing a comfortable and secure resting place above the ground out of the reach of snakes. Other hammocks could be used for suspending domestic equipment which consisted of carrying nets, gourds of large size used as containers, and of course the bundles of weapons used by the men. Their life of nomadic hunting was extremely hard, because in the environment of the tropical forests animals were scarce.

The Botocudo lived, mostly, from supplies of fish from the rivers, an occasional monkey from the trees and numbers of edible lizards. The amount of edible fruit in such forests is not great. These comparatively savage groups of Indians wandered round and round, always hunting for their subsistence, having little time for arts, no knowledge of the possibilities which agriculture would open to them, and no great need for any further domestic comforts. They did achieve a certain amount of decorative art, making head-dresses and collars from the feathers of tropical birds, and stringing teeth from various captured animals to make attractive necklaces and armlets. The men frequently pierced their lower lip and inserted studs which they polished out of bone or brightly coloured stone, and sometimes extra ones were put in the cheeks, making them hideous to our eyes but extremely

Below:
A late eighteenth-century French engraving of the Yahgan people of Tierra del Fuego. Although the treatment is thoroughly romantic the picture gave Europeans of the time an insight into the true conditions of Rousseau's theoretical noble savage.

Below, centre:
Botocudo Indians, a semi-nomadic people of the forests of eastern Brazil, as seen in the early nineteenth century. These hunting peoples had a sufficiently good living, through using weapons of wood and bone, to subsist without metal or stone tools. Note the wearing of large wooden plugs in the lower lips which was a distinguishing mark of these people. British Museum.

16

beautiful in the sight of their womenfolk who admired them as their protectors. The forcing of these ornaments through the sensitive mouth and cheek showed that they were capable of suffering pain – and so would be brave warriors and defend their families if attacked by any other group.

For them the world was filled with the spirits of the forests, creatures who could bring good or bad luck in hunting. They had little regard for the dead, who were usually just bundled up and left in the forest. Decomposition was quick; the little animals soon ate the flesh, and the bones were left lying around – perhaps some later hunter might find useful long bones to split into spear points. But there was little fear of the spirits of the dead and little regard for those who had left this world to go to the other hunting ground.

Sometimes the Botocudo Indians lived in rock shelters and shallow caves which happened to lie in the path of their wanderings. In these places they grouped together and were as thoroughly insanitary as our own ancestral hunters of the old Stone Age. The living quarters were at one side of the cave; on the other side all rubbish from the cooking, pieces of broiled meat, old bones, even the family toilets were all within a few steps of the general living quarters. A century and a half ago a traveller asked a group of the Botocudo why they lived in such conditions of dirt and evil smelling messiness. They replied that this was the smell of humanity and they liked it; if one went out into the forest there was the raw smell of wild animals and a feeling of constant danger, and what was unpleasant to the white man was to them the odour of homeliness, friendliness and comfort. It may be that this kind of thought was present in the minds of our distant ancestors

The Patagonian giants; an encampment of Tehuelche Indians seen on the voyage of the French navigator Dumont D'Urville in the early nineteenth century. The costume and skin *toldos* of the Patagonians had not changed since the sixteenth century when they were first observed. But the horse, introduced by Spanish settlers, had radically altered the basic culture of the tribes who had formerly subsisted by hunting on foot. British Museum.

Indian Woman of Florida
Water colour painting by
John White, 1587. The lady
is tattooed with bands of a
design found on ancient
pottery and shell objects in
Florida. She wears ear plugs,
and a single fringe of
brightly dyed fibre as her
only garment. The necklace
may have been presented to
her by her European visitors,
since she is obviously a lady
of high social rank. In one
hand she holds a gourd bowl
containing fruit, and in the
other what appear to be
prepared cakes of some kind.
Her nakedness was a normal
state and nobody would have
felt the least ashamed in a
community where life was
natural, if not simple.
British Museum.

Right:
A warrior of the same race,
though he is not in fact
dressed for battle. The bow is
for hunting, and the necklace
and loincloth the items he
would wear at a council.
Watercolour by John White,
1587. British Museum.

of 20,000 years ago, when they used the caves in France similarly –
both as habitation and as rubbish heaps.

There were few other Indians of the Americas who retained the
primitive hunting life. The Indians of the great plains – those famous
buffalo hunters of our childhood stories – were really agriculturalists
living near the river valleys. They cultivated little plantations of
maize and squash and they encouraged berry-bearing bushes and the
plants which grew near them. Hunting, it is true, was the mainstay
of their life, but they knew how to cultivate their own food.

In the pampas the Tehuelche had also for centuries practised a
little agriculture while remaining basically hunters. They caught
the wild guanaco and the flightless rhea – a bird somewhat like an
ostrich. These latter they caught by using the bolas, in which two
stone balls encased in rawhide were joined by a thong, anything from
three to six feet long; in the exact centre of this was a grip sometimes
also weighted with a stone. The bolas thrower set the stones whirling
above his head while holding the central grip, and when they had
achieved sufficient momentum he loosed the weapon at his quarry. It
promptly wrapped itself around the animal's legs, bringing it down.
The hunter could then finish off the creature with a spear or stone-
bladed hunting knife. The people moved within fairly limited hunting
ranges carrying with them enormous family tents made out of skins.
The great grassy plains of the pampas were rich in game and the
people had sufficient food to allow themselves some leisure. They spent
many hours scratching patterns on skin cloaks and on their living tents
and rubbing coloured ochres into them. These beautifully decorated
objects are quite rare in museums today but enough remain to show

18

Monument Valley. The 'totem pole' rock, when the sun is low in the sky, casts a shadow nearly thirty-five miles long.

us that the people of the pampas were not really primitive, though the small amount of agriculture that they practised was probably not of tremendous importance to them because of the ease with which they could keep themselves supplied with meat. One might say that the very success of their hunting contributed to their lack of progress.

The discovery of agriculture in ancient America seems to have begun in northern Mexico some 7-8,000 years ago, when a very primitive form of wild maize was utilized by bands of wandering hunters. This plant had only two small seeds rather like peas, quite unlike the great corn cobs of the modern maize plant. By careful nurture it was developed into a plant having small cobs about three inches long and probably containing about two ounces of grain. This early type of maize spread widely over Central America and into the southern United States, and provided the foundation for the later civilizations of middle America. The discovery must have been roughly of the same period as the discovery of agriculture in the Eurasian Middle East, but it was not accompanied in the early days of America by developments of large villages of the type of Jericho I in Palestine. The early maize cultivators appear to have been seasonal village dwellers, spending much of their year roaming the hunting grounds and gaining their food in the ancient way, but at certain seasons coming back to their villages and reaping the small crops which they had sown earlier in the year.

It could never have been a very rich life, but in this first appearance of sedentary living was the promise of all future tribal organization, domestic peace, and even the building of the brilliant culture that astonished the sixteenth-century European visitors.

19

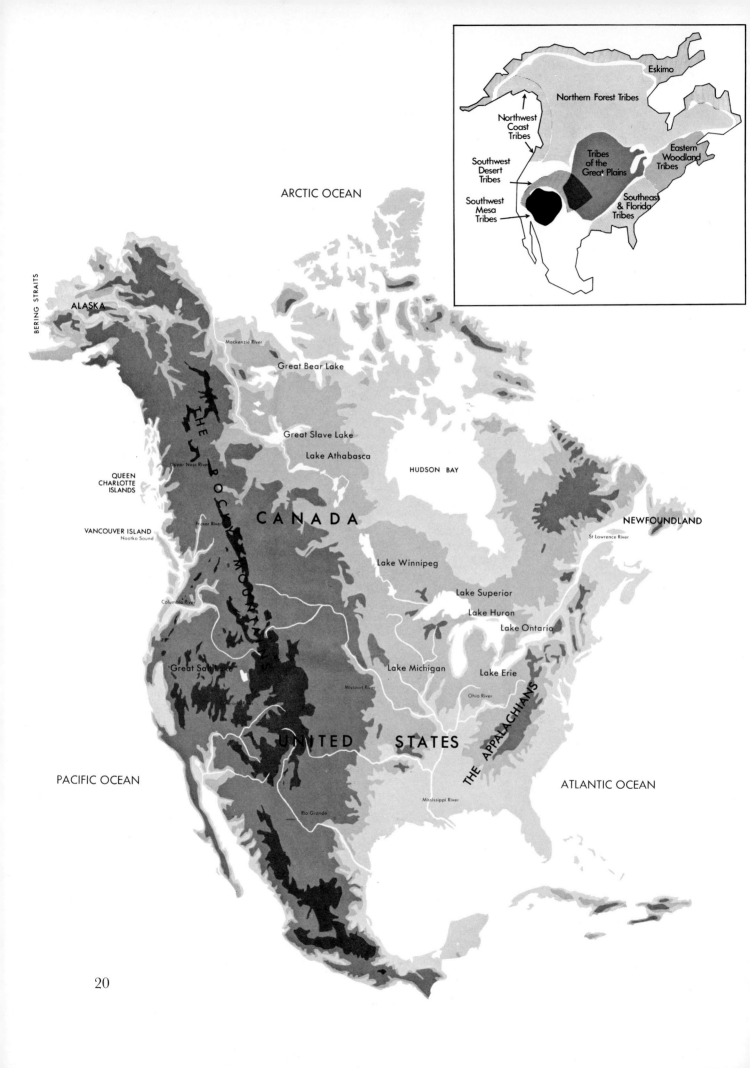

ARCTIC OCEAN

ALASKA

BERING STRAITS

Mackenzie River

Great Bear Lake

Great Slave Lake

Lake Athabasca

HUDSON BAY

QUEEN
CHARLOTTE
ISLANDS

Upper Nass River

CANADA

NEWFOUNDLAND

VANCOUVER ISLAND
Nootka Sound

Fraser River

St Lawrence River

Lake Winnipeg

Columbia River

THE ROCKY MOUNTAINS

Lake Superior

Lake Huron

Lake Ontario

Great Salt Lake

Lake Michigan

Lake Erie

Missouri River

Ohio River

Nevada Desert

UNITED   STATES

THE APPALACHIANS

PACIFIC OCEAN

Rio Grande

Mississippi River

ATLANTIC OCEAN

Eskimo

Northern Forest Tribes

Northwest
Coast
Tribes

Tribes
of the
Great Plains

Eastern
Woodland
Tribes

Southwest
Desert
Tribes

Southwest
Mesa
Tribes

Southeast
& Florida
Tribes

20

Northwest Coast Indians

Carved grip of a wooden implement of the Haida Indians of British Columbia. This represents adventures of the mythological hero Raven. The profile face below shows him as a man within the killer whale which has seized him. Later he emerges in the form of a dragon fly. Late eighteenth century.

The Indians of British Columbia, southern Alaska and the coast of Oregon present an interesting problem to archaeologists. When discovered by European voyagers in the late eighteenth century they were people of an advanced neolithic culture, using polished stone implements, and living in fixed villages without agriculture. Food was plentiful: every year immense numbers of salmon and kindred fish came in from the Pacific, swimming up river to their spawning grounds. This in itself was an inexhaustible seasonal food supply and the seas were also rich in other types of fish and sea mammal. Inland there were considerable numbers of bear, some varieties of deer, and a few caribou. At no time of the year would there be a total absence of food supplies – the animals were nonmigratory – and the migratory fish were successfully treated by simple methods of food preservation. At the right seasons of the year wild berries, several kinds of edible roots and green leaves were available; so that there was a naturally balanced diet with good supplies of vitamins. The great forests provided cedar trees, the roots of which could be pounded to make a useful textile.

We do not know how long the particular culture of these groups of Northwest Coast Indians existed. Stone bowls and occasional stone blades, which are carbon dated at some fifteen centuries ago, show that their technology had changed little by the time these Indians were first visited by Captains Cook and Vancouver. The only really modern development in their culture has been the huge totem pole, which in early days had simply been a door post to a house and never rose above the level of the eaves. But in the early nineteenth century the fur trade soon made it possible for the native peoples to acquire considerable wealth through hunting. Seal, otter and beaver skins were sold to the white man in enormous quantities in return not only for guns and traps but also for steel tools, so that the Indian carver equipped with the newly imported chisels and axes of steel, was able to enlarge the scale of his previous work and produce huge carvings.

The curious feature about this hunting and fishing culture was that there was no need to move one's habitation. People didn't have to go far to find animals, and plentiful supplies of fish were to be obtained locally. With their fine equipment of stone tools the Indians were able to carve themselves large dugout canoes, some of which were eighty feet long and eight feet broad, beautifully shaped with

21

Previous page :
A modern multi-storey
Pueblo Indian house block.
The woman in the fore-
ground is married, and wears
a black cloth which derives
ultimately from contact with
Spanish tradition when the
Pueblos were part of Mexico.
Note the projecting roof
beams through the adobe
walls; the access ladders for
higher storeys. The modern
doorways and framed win-
dows show how the Pueblo
Indians are adapting to
modern life without
altogether abandoning their
ancient culture.

An Indian encampment for
the summer fishing on the
Northwest Coast of America.
The artist had some difficulty
with the unusual shape of the
dug-out canoe on the left.
The woman with a bundle on
her back is bringing in
spruce roots which will later
be pounded to extract the
soft fibres which were woven
into garments. This picture
was made on the late
eighteenth century voyage of
the French navigator La
Perouse.

carefully carved bows for shearing the water. These were propelled
by paddles and were thoroughly seaworthy craft. The various
islands of the Queen Charlotte group were constantly in contact.
Several branches of the Haida tribe lived there, and whether feuding
or exchanging materials in peace there was constant need for inter-
island contact. The tribes living along the mainland coast were also
good seamen. They went whale hunting on the ocean many miles
from shore and made long voyages from place to place, both for
raiding and trading. This was all necessary mobility, but when
people returned to base they liked to have their village on an easily
defensible piece of rising ground near a good salmon river and within
easy reach of the sea.

Each tribal group examined the area available to them very, very
carefully and chose their living sites with the cautious eyes of some
medieval prince. Their palisaded village was very much their castle.
Their access to the sea was also their access to the roads of trade and
basic supply. Within this economy there was no need for agriculture.

This way of life allowed for periods of leisure and the production
of works of art. The beliefs of the Northwest Coast Indians centred
on their ancestors and their immediate environment, and these were
honoured in ceremonies resembling mystery plays. The actors wore
elaborately carved masks representing the spirits of nature and the
ancestors of the various clans, and some of this work is remarkable.
The skill of the woodcarvers has already been mentioned and in
addition they made use of shell, ivory, the feathers of sea birds,
raw copper, and argillite.

Big village communities had a centralized social system arranged

in a pyramidal hierarchy, at the top of which were the chiefs of the clans. These carried the responsibility of organizing the life of the tribe, and the fishing and hunting which provided the food. Below them were the ordinary householders, and then the slaves, who were mostly prisoners of war captured from other tribes. Each chief was the head of a clan whose visible symbol of unity was the totem.

Totemism was not the belief that these people had descended from strange animal ancestors. (although their mythology sometimes included such stories), but a division of society according to animal crests. The Indians of the Northwest Coast used totems in much the same way as the medieval Europeans used heraldic crests. The Earls of Warwick used a bear and ragged staff as a distinguishing symbol for themselves, their kinsmen and their followers, in exactly the same way as the members of the bear totem were using their symbol when they put it on their houses, their personal equipment and on all the utensils of their household. Totemic crests were carved on houseposts above the central doorway, and in later times, when the Indians had obtained fine steel tools, larger carvings were made. In particular, the totem pole at the entrance to a house showed the totems of three generations in the owner's family. This display of totems had a very practical purpose: visitors would observe these symbols on the house and go straight to one that represented their own totem. A bear or raven on a house meant that the owner had acknowledged relationship with all other members of the bear or raven clan. He was obliged to give any of them hospitality without counting the cost.

Likewise, if he went to their village, he was treated as one of the family even if he had come from a couple of hundred miles away and

The great totem poles of the mid-nineteenth century were only carved in the period when the fur trade brought wealth and metal tools to the Indians, who in more ancient times of stone tools carved posts only up to ten feet in height as part of the entrance to their wooden houses.

Left:
Carved wooden mask of the Haida Indians of Queen Charlotte Islands, British Columbia. This delicately wrought work with its polychrome painting represents a spirit, part dragon-fly and part bear, and was worn at the winter festivals. The masker had a narrow field of vision provided through the nostrils. London Missionary Society Collection.

25

26

Northwest Coast Indians

had never met any of the individuals before. In most of the more important activities of life the idea of kinship between members of the totem was quite important. Each individual success was to the credit of the whole clan.

The mythology of the Northwest Coast contains many stories about the various totem animals and their relationship to humans. A good example is the myth of the bear totem. The heroine, the aristocratic and enormously self-important eldest daughter of a village chief, offended the bears by complaining loud and long when she stepped in some bear's excrement in the woods. She was so full of anger for these filthy animals that when she later met a charming young prince in the same woods, it never occurred to her that he might be one of the bear people. The prince took her to his splendid home and made her his wife. The house was full of all kinds of fine food, the prince's family were genial, and it took the girl a long time to realize that the people she was living with became animals when they donned

27

bearskins and left their home. Nevertheless, she lived with the bear people quite happily for a long time—long enough to have two fine children. Then one day the girl heard the barking of dogs and looked out of the cave to see her two brothers searching for her.

Her father-in-law heard the dogs, too, and he knew what must happen. He came to her and begged her to kill him so that she should have freedom and that her children would be received among the children of men. No sooner was he killed than the whole beautiful house turned into a cave that had obviously been inhabited by bears. The bear prince and all his kinsmen were wild bears and were only like human beings in spirit. The girl had learned to see through the animal form and understood that, in spirit, the bears lived in a wonderful and beautiful world. But with the howling of the dogs from the world outside, this world was lost. Her children later achieved good positions in the tribe and were famed for their quiet, cautious wisdom and their ability to bring home plenty of food for their families. They had something of the patient, capable spirit of the bears of the wood, and were the ancestors of all the members of the Bear totem.

Like many other Indian myths, this one links the characters of people with what people have observed as the characters of animals. We use the same sort of link when we say that someone is a vixen, or a sheep, or even a silly donkey. Life in a Northwest Coast village, which sometimes included over a thousand individuals, was richly varied. Every village contained members of several different totem groups who inter-married according to a set pattern. One could not marry a member of one's own totem, but had to marry a member of one of two or three affiliated groups. So a family usually had more than one totem affiliation, and these were very useful for building a sense of unity between the different groups.

Often a tribe only covered the territories of a dozen or so villages, but their strong sense of unity—which was largely a unity of language—brought them together to combat other tribes in raids and wars. There were differences in dialects, but there was not much difference in culture between any of the tribal groups. One can sometimes distinguish between the art work of the Haida and other tribes, like the Tsimshian, because the Haida artists created a style of great delicacy, and the Tsimshian preferred large surfaces and bold design. But the tribes all hunted the same kind of animals, held the same kind of ceremonies, and lived in similar houses. They were often rivals in the fishing and hunting grounds, and it was very difficult for them not to attribute the quarrels which arose to an imagined difference in race. In such a savage society the concept of an over-riding cultural unity simply did not exist. It was far away in the eastern part of the United States, sometime in the sixteenth century, that the Lone Pine chief, Hiawatha, brought the six major tribes of the Iroquois into a confederation. But the good sense of such a confederation was not accessible to the non-agricultural people of the Northwest Coast, and they remained separated even when they became part of the modern world.

Neolithic life, using heavy stone tools and the advanced technology which make settled village life possible, seems to have been independently discovered by these Indians. It is most unusual for a people living by hunting and fishing to tackle the problems of building big houses and constructing large dug-out canoes. Most hunting tribes

Haida Indian carving in argillite from Queen Charlotte Islands, British Columbia. This represents a totem pole showing a family's ancestral crests. The present chief is of the Eagle totem, descended from Raven, Bear-Mother, and Earth Frog. Late nineteenth century.

28

have to keep the forests intact, since woodlands are the places where game is always to be found. Since the weapons of the chase have to be provided with comparatively light stone points adapted for piercing, there seemed no reason for making any large or heavy implements at all. In the Northwest Coast region the population grew to fairly large numbers because of the general abundance of food in the area. A cultural problem must have been proposed to them through internal warfare. Sometimes a large group of attacking warriors had to be held off. This demanded the construction of fairly heavy palisades and of large and strong houses which finally became something like fortresses. There was an incentive for inventing fairly large tools for chopping down trees just for this particular purpose.

At a very early stage, someone must have seen large tree trunks washed down the rivers after storms and made the logical step of considering the advantages of such large timber for the construction of boats. However it began, the art of making beautiful and big canoes developed quickly among these Indians. The prow, shaped to cut the water, and the rather high bows remind one in a vague way of East Asian construction. It is true that occasionally Japanese fishermen crossed the North Pacific and visited these coasts, long before any European or Russian voyagers had been there. It may be that there was some direct influence, although the native method of cutting a dug-out from a single tree has practically no technical relationship to the plank-built boats of the Asian fishermen.

Work on the large dug-out meant the use of heavy adzes, which were necessary to take long slices of wood out of the central cavity. Even though the Indians used fire to soften the surface along the centre, it was still a great advantage to have quite heavy sharp-edged tools for swinging at the charred wood and then breaking off strips of wood between the areas of two small fires. The general shape of an implement is conditioned by its function and by the material available. There was plenty of good hard stone and strong springy wood, so the Indians soon learned to find a strong joint or fork of tree boughs, and then lash the blade to one of them, using the longer one as the handle. There is a high probability that the shape of heavy wood-working adzes in any part of the world will be somewhat similar. Although it is not impossible, it is definitely not necessary that there should have been any contact between Polynesian voyagers who used similar implements for their carving and the Indians of

Wooden wolf mask of the Haida Indians. The eyes are inlaid with abalone shell, and the mouth is filled with seal teeth. The soft leather straps served to secure it to the head of an actor who was able to see through the open mouth, while taking part in the winter plays. Late eighteenth century.

29

Monument Valley in early twilight. This famous physical feature of south-east Utah is the result of millennia of erosion, the red sandstone formations appearing to rise up starkly from the floor of the valley.

Far right:
Dakota (Sioux) painting on prepared deer skin. This represents a vision of the spirits in the sky. The houses in the sky are bigger and better, and there the sun and moon have their abode. It is the place whence prayers go through the eagle-feather fringed pipe stems. The vision is of a great medicine man leading the horned manitou in a dance, warriors among them. They danced as the aurora dances in winter evenings.

30

the Northwest Coast. In any case the sea currents and the prevailing winds were against such contacts. So one must feel that in this area the development of heavy stone tools and strong wooden buildings were connected solely with local conditions.

The Indians of the Northwest Coast followed a social pattern that seems to have been common to many other peoples in other parts of the world. The more complicated social structure that develops when a nomadic culture becomes a culture of fixed villages, invested many village chiefs with varying amounts of power. This situation led to conflicts between neighbouring tribal chiefs and then to the organization of raiding parties, the raids developed into small-scale wars that necessitated the building of defensive structures around the villages. Something like this also happened in the Polynesian islands; and it seems that a similar development occurred in Europe during the Bronze Age. There is no record at all of the Indians of the Northwest Coast of America ever having planted grain or deliberately grown vegetables. But there was no reason for them to turn to agriculture, since their vegetable foods were merely a supplement to fishing and hunting. They knew how to preserve fish for periods of scarcity and for the season when the salmon were not swimming up the rivers. Salmon were split and dried on light wooden frames over a slow fire; in this process some of the rich oil dropped from them and was collected in wooden vessels. Also the livers of the fish were very carefully pressed to extract the oil. Wooden oil containers were usually

The flat roofs of the Zuñi pueblos. In the foreground is a heap of wet clay ready for making the sun-dried adobe blocks from which these desert houses are made. The roofs as can be seen are often used as workshops and one can see where a woman has been making pots and another has been hulling her maize. Beyond the roofs is the flood plain of a desert stream which gives sufficient moisture to enable the townspeople to survive in conditions of some comfort. Photo by J. K. Hillers, 1879.

beautifully carved, and through constant use through the ages became so impregnated with the oil that they were completely waterproof and could be relied on to preserve oil almost indefinitely.

It may seem strange that people should attach great importance to a substance that we might consider unpalatable. But for the Indians this oil had a very important function; they dipped their dried fish into it and then ate it, without knowing that the oil was reinforcing their supplies of vitamins and so building up their health when berries and greenstuffs were not easily available. There is no record to show that there were plagues, pestilences or any other outbreaks of illness of great extent among the people. Their dependence on the salmon was no hindrance to the general state of their well-being. But on the whole the fact that both dried flesh and stored oil were available meant that in the long nights of winter all manner of social ceremonies could be carried on. Dances illustrating folk-lore and ceremonies for the installation of chiefs and the reception of visitors were held. Between the periods of preparing food the women had a good deal of leisure which they used to twine beautiful cloaks and capes from the firm, flexible and warm fibre made from pounded cedar roots. Some of the better robes were decorated with a thick woolly twist made of the very fine wool-like hair combed from the backs of their dogs, which were rather like huskies in appearance.

Women lived a comparatively free life. They held their own position in society, not only as wives and mothers, but as the people who made clothing, and the people through whom the chief counted his descent as much as from his father's side. Some tribes in fact counted all their descent in the female line. Considerable honour was paid to elderly women, who were regarded as the repositories of wisdom and were the great story tellers who passed on the lore and history of their ancestors. In fact this Stone Age fishing civilization reached considerable heights of development and must be looked on as a unique phenomenon in human history.

The First Farmers

Agriculture in the Americas started about 9,000 years ago, not very far distant in time from the first farming in the Old World. However, the grains developed were entirely different. Within the Americas there were no edible grasses such as wheat, oats or barley, nor was there any true rice. The basic grain developed was maize, first cultivated in Mexico. Quinoa seems to have been cultivated even before maize in Peru, where maize found its way from the north.

The true home of maize seems to have been northern Mexico and the southwestern United States, where the original plant, now totally extinct, was a small grass bearing two seeds only; each of these was like a rather small single grain of modern maize. In the progress of centuries of cultivation the plant lost its power of self-reproduction and it is now entirely dependant on human agency for its fertilization and development. In a few centuries the little wild plant had been so improved by careful husbandry that it was producing small cobs, about the size of a human thumb, containing about thirty or forty grains of good, nourishing starch food. Archaeology has shown that the development of the maize plant in north-west Mexico was accompanied by development in housing. At the very beginning of cultivation attention to the fields was only seasonal, villages were very temporary and contained only a few flimsy huts. It seems that a patch of ground was dug over, the maize was planted and then the people would move away and spend a period in hunting, only returning when it was time to reap the crop, to prepare packs of tortillas for eating and to select the seed grain ready for the next planting season. This very simple agriculture was slowly developed until it became possible for people to live all the year round in a fixed village. They kept regular supplies of maize in great baskets near their houses and added to their food by local hunting, and the gathering of wild or semi-cultivated food plants. These other food plants included various types of bean and many plants of the squash family.

We have no clue to the rate of the spread of maize cultivation from one tribe to another. It reached Peru as early as 1,000 B.C. In the other direction there were vague traditions that maize came from the south to the North American Indian tribes in the area of the Great Lakes, but that must have been nearly 2,000 years ago. By the time Europeans had arrived cultivated maize was known from the Great Lakes region (farther north the winters were too cold) right

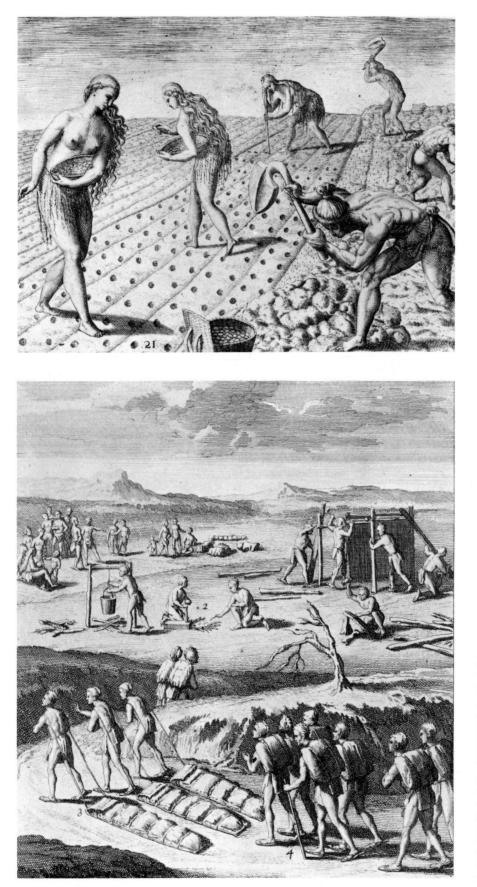

Indians of Florida planting maize in the early seventeenth century. Note the men use the heavy wooden hoes to prepare the ground, and the women pierce the ground and plant the seed. The carrying basket in the foreground is a practical solution to the problem of carrying heavy loads easily, and has parallels all over the world. The women wear only a fringe of fibre, and there is evidence that this was often dyed blue, setting off their pale brown skin rather beautifully. The loin-cloth of the men was a type of costume common from Panama to New England in early times. From De Bry, *Historia Americae sivi Novi Orbis,* 1634.

Indians of the eastern woodlands of Canada, probably Hurons. Traders drag sledges or carry packs on their backs. A man splits wood with a deer-bone cleaver. Fire is made by rotating a hard fire-stick on a soft-wood block, and maple syrup is boiled in a wooden bucket. The framework in the background is the beginning of a wigwam which will be covered by sheets of bark. The general absence of clothing is quite characteristic of Indian tribes, shown in all pictures of this early period. From the late eighteenth-century *Moeurs des Sauvages,* Paris.

34

down to the pampas of Argentina. Some small groups of really
primitive hunting people had no use for it, but that is because maize in
its cultivated state has to be cared for by the farmer and does not grow
wild. For this reason the Tehuelches and the Fuegians had no
knowledge of maize. Some of the smaller tribes of the desert regions of
California who used wild acorns as their main source of starch food
also practised no formal agriculture. Within the tropical forest
areas of America root plants, such as the cassava and manioc were
more easily cultivated than maize. But this refers almost entirely to the
South American forest areas of the Amazon and the Orinoco. In the
forested regions of southern Mexico the Maya people cultivated maize
in roughly prepared forest clearings and they found no real difficulty
in the process. The main spread of maize into South America was
along the mountain ranges, and it is probable that the forest people
had discovered their root crops long before maize had been introduced
to the highlands.

In the Andes, particularly in the more civilized areas, the potato
was grown. Many varieties of it were developed, and many ways of
preparing it were known, including frozen potato powder which the
natives of the Andes used to make a basically nourishing gruel that
could be augmented by adding pieces of meat.

The practice of agriculture, as we have seen, had tended to anchor
people to their own neighbourhood. The farmer could not leave his
fields for too long, or at least his wife and family could not do so
because they were constantly employed in watching over the fields.
They drove away rats and birds and kept the place clean, so that the
majority of the food grown was available for human rather than animal
consumption. This was a vital social step. There was now a fixed
home in which the children could be reared near their mother. There
was no necessity to leave on constant nomadic journeys in search of
the food animals or for new areas in which one could find edible plants.
With the settlement in permanent homes after the development of
agriculture came the invention of pottery. This development is
paralleled in the Old World, as seen in sites such as that of Jericho
where there is evidence of cultivation of food stuffs and animal
husbandry on small homesteads before there was any pottery.

Early methods of agriculture persisted throughout the American
continent. In most areas cultivation was simply a matter of placing
seeds into a hole made by a digging stick. There was no attempt to
use manure or artificial fertilizer of any kind. As a consequence the
ground gradually became exhausted and people moved to a new plot.
This was then covered with ash of burnt grass, or burnt wood, and
simply replanted. The new crops would continue to flourish over two
or three years, and after that one would move to another patch of
ground. In general the procedure was to return to the original plot
some twenty or thirty years after it had been lying fallow, so that the
fertility of the soil was regained and the wild vegetation which had
sprung up produced a natural fertilizer when it was burnt down. This
system of shifting cultivation was perfectly sufficient for smallish
groups of people. The garden plots would be moved in a circuit round
a fixed village. In some cases, particularly in the heavily forested
areas in South America, the village, usually only one large communal
house, would deteriorate in time and be rebuilt near whatever cultivation plot was then in use. But such tribes moved in very restricted areas.

35

The First Farmers

In North America there was considerable cultivation in the Great Plains wherever a river valley gave shelter from the winter winds, and the crops of beans, squash and maize could be grown to best effect. Before A.D. 1600 while the Indians still hunted on foot, these garden plots produced a regular basic food supply. There was a certain amount of shifting up and down the river, and in some historic cases whole villages were moved from site to site so that over a century they would ascend rivers for a matter of fifty to a hundred miles. Always, however, the river valley was in reach of the prairie, parts of which were regarded as the tribal hunting grounds. The main body of the tribe would split up during the hunting season into groups which would gather meat from the buffalo herds as they arrived. Every year towards the end of the migration there was a communal buffalo hunt in which groups of the animals were cut off from the herd, surrounded and killed. The meat was air dried, on wooden frames. The fat was beaten up with wild berries to make pemmican. This nourishing foodstuff was packed into specially tanned leather containers, known to us as *parfleche*. These could be taken to the home village and hung inside the houses. Such homes were frequently quite large structures, framed in wood and covered with sods of earth until they looked like natural hills with a smoke hole in the centre. Some earth houses were sixty feet across and could contain not only three or four related families but also the dogs of the people living there.

The simple agriculture of the Plains Indians was far surpassed by the organized farming of the Indians of the eastern parts of the U.S.A. The villages of the Iroquois were defended by palisades and usually stood on a bluff above a river so that there was easy access to the water – as well as possibilities of defence in case of attack. Around the village were fixed areas in which maize was grown, and there

Indians of Virginia making dug-out canoes. The tree is ringed with fire to enable easy felling, and the branches and bark are peeled off. The dried bole is charred by small fires and cleaned out by a stone gouge without a haft. Note the hair of the men, a fashion which persisted until a century ago. From De Bry, *Historia Americae sivi Novi Orbis*, 1634.

A Mandan burial ground on the prairie. The two skin-covered objects are medicine bags containing relics and charms through which the Indian can come into contact with the spirit world. The racks in the background are frames on which the bodies of the dead lie wrapped in skins under the sky. On the right is the Mandan winter village of semi-subterranean houses covered by mounds of earth with a smoke hole on top. Painted for Maximilian Prinz zu Wied by Carl Bodmer in 1832-1834. Published in *Travels in North America* in 1843.

36

The First Farmers

were also quite well cultivated apple orchards. Often the village
was purposely built within easy reach of large stands of sugar maple,
which were tapped at the appropriate season. The flowing juice
would be taken and boiled to produce a sweet and nourishing syrup.
Fishing on rivers and lakes was highly organized, and elaborate
palisaded fish weirs, fitted with basketry traps to catch the smaller
fish, were in common use. This organized method of farming and
fishing meant that there was a reasonably stable food supply and large
villages of people could live and work together in a communal way
without undue expenditure of time and energy in obtaining the basic
necessities.

Between the various tribal units within the confederacy there were
great areas of uncultivated woodland. Communal hunts were
arranged in these. Sometimes small towns would combine to fix long
rows of palisades enclosing a triangular area of forest. Alongside
these, at one end, the women and children of the tribe would create
a disturbance, shouting, waving skins, beating on trees with pieces of
wood and scaring the animals. The animals, rushing forward, found
palisades blocking their way on either side which gradually led them
closer and closer to a narrow opening and this in turn led to a corral.
The terrified animals rapidly filled the corral where they were shot
or speared by the warriors. Some might escape but even then there were
rows of spring traps and pit traps arranged so that a good proportion
of them would be caught. The skins were tanned and were very
useful for clothing and decoration. Deer skin in particular was
smoked over a wooden fire after the hairs had been scraped off. It was
rubbed with ash, lime and fat, scraped and rescraped and resmoked
until finally one had beautiful, supple material which would make an
almost waterproof garment. At first it seems that these clothes

A sun dance lodge as seen
among the Mandans in the
eighteen-forties by George
Catlin. In the centre by the
hearth the Medicine Man
calls upon the Power Above
(The Great Spirit) to
strengthen the young war-
riors who have fasted for
three days before this with
their shields and arms hung
behind them in peace. On
the fourth day they will join
the Medicine Man in danc-
ing and chanting to the
music of the four drums lying on the ground. After-
wards they will submit to
painful tortures such as running round the lodge with
heavy buffalo skulls attached
to them by skewers stuck
through their flesh. They will
hope to receive visions which
will give them protective
guardian spirits for the rest
of their lives.

consisted only of little soft aprons and a cape which could be hung over the shoulder. Important people wore long capes reaching from shoulder to ankle. Women sometimes wore elaborate and very pretty fringes, which draped from one shoulder over to the hip bone on the other side and hung down in an open fringe of about eight or nine inches in depth; this was dyed in bright colours and made a rather graceful ornament. Thus organized hunting not only provided a useful supply of meat, but also the basic clothing. The farms produced enough vegetables for food and the rivers gave fish.

The organization of these farming tribes became big enough for a system of recording events to become important. This was done by the use of wampum. Wampum was made of tubular beads of either purple or white – made from the hinges of a spondylus shell. On any great occasion strings of these beads were threaded, and sometimes woven into elaborately decorated belts. These were given to professional Keepers of the Wampum, whose duty it was every year to bring out the belts and recite the story of the event which they were made to commemorate. Such a belt still in existence records William Penn's purchase of the land which was the nucleus of Pennsylvania. Others record small family events; a happy event was signified by a single short strand of white beads; a bereavement by a short string of purple beads, but only professionally trained men knew the meaning. For others the significance was not immediately apparent, and even when there was a pattern they could not decipher it. In one large belt, now in London, there are three wide oblongs in white on a purple belt signifying death or war; the centre one is larger than the others and has four corners. It is only because it is known that it was probably of Delaware Indian origin that one can deduce that the three squares represent the council huts of the three totemic groups of the Delaware Indians. The large centre one with its four corners emphasized represents the turtle clan – with the corners showing the four feet of the animal sticking beyond its shell. But nobody except the official Keeper of the Wampum would be quite sure of this or able to say on what occasion this belt was made.

It happens that it is threaded on yellow French silk and it may well be that this was the belt presented by the French to encourage the Delaware to fight against the British settlers of North America. By means of such records, recited at the annual gathering of the whole tribe, the Iroquois people had knowledge of their history which went back for three or four centuries at least, and may possibly have gone beyond. Some belts had a special meaning as vehicles of mythology; and it was from the recital which was made when the belts were displayed that people learnt about the spirits of the wind and the rain and the storm. Some told of the necessity for the young men to dance in masks at certain seasons to frighten away evil spirits from the crops, or of the reasons for the women to walk naked around the fields when the corn was newly planted – in order that their feminine power of reproduction should infect the corn and give it new strength and new life. This was also an ancient custom in some parts of Europe, presumably with the same purpose, but it would be quite unwise to assume that there was any material contact which had introduced an Indian custom to Europe – or a European folk custom to the Americas.

In areas farther to the south the development of civilization was going on at a rather more accelerated pace. In the Appalachians,

Far left, above:
Indian warriors of Virginia, probably of the Powhatan group, visited by John White in 1587. They were speakers of an Algonquian language, and lived by farming garden plots, and by hunting. Behind the two warriors a deer hunt is in progress. American Indian costume of this period consisted of a fringed and tailed leather apron, beads of shell and copper armlets. Engraving from the De Bry, *Historia Americae siva Novi Orbis;* 1634.

Far left, below:
The town of Pomeiock in about 1587, as drawn by John White. This is an American Indian village of a type once well known in neolithic Europe. It is defended by a stockade, and the village meeting place is in the centre. These bark-covered houses were known as wigwams, and as can be seen they are very different from the skin tipis of the Plains Indians. British Museum.

Mohegan Indian wooden ladle with the figure of a woman carved on the handle. This is an exceedingly rare object, one of the very few surviving examples of the sculpture of the eastern woodland tribes of America. The dress of the figure, a leather skirt and basketry cap is not otherwise known. New York State, seventeenth century. Van Rensslaer family collection.

especially in the southern part of the ranges, tribes such as the Cherokee were building towns beside the track-ways, usually a single row of large cabins, among which would be raised platforms containing temples of the various nature gods and large houses for the chiefs and tribal elders.

Around the mouth of the Mississippi there was an ancient and elaborate social organization as late as the seventeenth century among the Natchez whose chiefs and priests were an aristocratic social class. There were also citizens, second-class citizens, and a certain number of slaves. The gods were worshipped with elaborate ceremonial performed before images of wood and clay in their temples. The more primitive type of medicine-man here became a priest whose religious dances were aimed at making contact with the divine spirit, bringing health to the sick, blessing to the crops, and prosperity to the nation. The tribal towns at the time of discovery by Europeans were quite large, some of them having a population of at least 1,000 warriors, so the population of a good-sized Natchez town would probably have been in the neighbourhood of 3,000 individuals. In the seventeenth century, however, the community was past its first strength, and was now subject to pressure by surrounding tribes, so that we must conclude that in earlier times it had been larger and more powerful.

It is by no means certain but it is possible that the Natchez were directly related to the builders of the Hopewell and Adena Mound cultures of the middle Mississippi and the Ohio valleys. Here from the second century B.C. up to the sixth or seventh century A.D. there were people who made good quality coiled pottery, and used raw copper hammered into elaborate personal ornaments. Their artists incised pictures showing both gods and warriors on shells which were worn as decoration. They were skilled carvers in stone, making images and beautiful pipe bowls for smoking tobacco.

These people erected their most important buildings on earthen mounds which sometimes have the form of enormous animals, probably representing constellations or else the great water spirits in the form of serpents which were so common in American Indian legend. We know nothing of their social organisation but they quite obviously included a special warrior caste and important religious leaders. Warriors are shown holding the heads of slain enemies. Presumably there was an honour cult in which the whole human head was treated much as the Indians of the Plains used the scalps of their enemy as decorations to show their great prowess in war.

No doubt there was an extensive and well planned agricultural system to support this type of civilization but there are, as far as we know, no traces from which we can estimate the size of fields or the rotation of crops. The people made great quantities of large flat stone blades which appear to be hoe blades for breaking up the soil. From the perfection of the workmanship on these objects we can be quite sure that agriculture had a very important place, and was considered worthy of the expenditure of considerable time and patience in perfecting its implements. The immense number of tobacco pipes carved in the form of birds, animals and human heads, tell us of the artistic skill and exact observation of nature which the carvers possessed. Possibly they represent totem animals of some kind, or perhaps even the animals from their mythology. Some carvings

Stone figure of a frog used as a tobacco pipe. This was excavated from a mound in Boone County, Kentucky, and belongs to the early centuries A.D. It probably represents the frog as a symbol of the Earth Mother. British Museum.

illustrate stories – the primitive equivalent of books of religious and historical information.

In South America we find that something a little more advanced was developed in northern Argentina where the Diaguita and Calchaqui had not only organized farming, but kept herds of semi-wild llamas for a regular food supply. They built smallish houses from rough blocks of stone on small mounds. The tribes could form confederacies of several towns, and bring to bear large armies which presented a threat to the Inca empire in Peru. This led eventually to the final Inca conquest of most of their towns in what is now northern Chile, in the fifteenth century.

The Diaguita farther south made themselves a very good living by fishing as well as farming. They made elaborate and very beautiful pottery, and in fact brought a more advanced civilization to the tribes who for untold centuries had inhabited the coastlands.

The coastal regions of Chile acquired a small amount of culture, simple pottery and weaving mostly, from occasional contacts with the people to the north in what is now Peru, but they were basically Stone Age fisher folk living as their northern neighbours had done two millennia earlier. As one followed the country southwards the level of civilization decreased, and in southern Chile and Magellan's Straits the simple tribespeople existed for millennia in a most primitive way on shellfish and seal hunting.

To the east of Peru, but south of the great forests, were many related tribes of Indians. In some ways these were nearly as accomplished as the Diaguita, though they seem never to have advanced beyond simple village life. There is no evidence that any of them lived together in sufficient numbers to build a town or form a state which controlled other tribes. Their descendants are the Indians of the Paraguayan Chaco. All of them could make useful pottery, and all used polished stone tools. They had learned weaving from contact with the Peruvians, but their restricted agriculture had to be helped out by hunting.

Once in the past, probably most importantly in the tenth to twelfth centuries A.D. they had been more settled, and probably had more extensive areas of cultivation. Their pottery was then very competently made, and included huge painted urns which were, like the big Diaguita urns, used as sarcophagi for burying children. The discovery of such urns, and the remains of the chain of Inca forts guarding the foothills of the Andes, led to the circulation of stories of another lost civilization which led explorers including the famous Colonel Fawcett to adventure into these wild and desolate regions of South America. It may even be that native folk tales preserved memories of the days when the Inca armies were on the frontiers, telling of the wealthy land of gold beyond the borders.

Parallel in culture with the Diaguita were the Indians of the south-west area of the United States and northern Mexico. In early times, about the beginning of the Christian era, these people also lived in small villages. Sometimes in later centuries a whole village was built as a single house made up of adobe blocks stuck together. A wooden framework was built in to support floors or ceilings. Some of these houses were three storeys high. The location of villages was associated with irrigation strips for cultivation along the river beds. As time went on social organization among the varied tribes became more

Tobacco pipes carved from steatite. These ancient pipes dating from the beginning of the Christian era come from the Adena and Hopewellian cultures of the middle Mississippi and Ohio Valleys. They represent both mythological and realistic concepts but were probably used only for semi-religious ritual smoking. Squier and Davis Collection.

41

complex. The group-buildings sometimes became enormous mansions, some containing several hundred rooms on six or seven storeys. In the courtyards were circular pits sunk below ground level, and roofed over. Here the men conducted ceremonies in honour of the gods and spirits. These were the originals of the Kivas, which were the sacred places of the Pueblo Indians of recent times.

It happened in the American south-west that climatic changes caused a progressive aridity. In the tenth and eleventh centuries rivers dried up, and former grasslands became stony deserts. The people on the edge of the plains, buffalo hunting tribes such as the Tejas, after whom the state of Texas was named, were forced to seek more food. They made occasional desperate raids into the agricultural lands of more civilized neighbours. This induced the various groups of agriculturalists to rebuild their homes in caves or high up on the flat tops of the mesas in that part of the country. From their safe refuge they could lure parties of raiders into the valley below and then cut them off. In this way they succeeded in holding raiding parties from the Plains at bay, while the people went down from their highland towns to farm small plots of land. Wherever there was a sign of water, where a stream bed ran which for one or two months of the year actually contained water, there these Indians of the towns—the Pueblo Indians—managed to grow very successful crops. They cultivated plantations of fruit trees as well as areas devoted to the more succulent varieties of gourd and squash. Maize was, of course, their staple food. They brought the ripe cobs home on the long climb up the hills to their houses, where maize was kept in enormous clay bins.

Indians of Florida, probably Seminoles, of the late sixteenth century. The hut had mud-plastered walls over a light wooden framework. The large canoe has been dug out of a tree trunk, by scraping with stone blades after small fires had been lit along its length. The lack of clothing was characteristic of most American Indians in pre-European times. Engraving from De Bry, *Historia Americae sivi Novi Orbis*, 1634.

42

The First Farmers

The Pueblos were run by councils under the leadership of clan chiefs, but since these towns were by nature collections of refugees coming originally from several different tribal groups they had a very democratic structure. This spirit was not expressed in a voting system, but through discussion in the various societies to which the men belonged. They worshipped the ancestors and the powers of nature, and were organized into many societies with special functions, meeting regularly in the circular underground Kivas to hold their ceremonies. In these meetings people could and did express opinions about the government and the organization of their towns. Since each society covered a considerable part of the male population it was possible for them to exert real pressure upon those chiefs who were members of their religious club.

At certain times of the year the societies would parade, wearing masks, and dancing through the town. They brought good fortune from the spirit world by dancing with the masks of the spirits. They gave blessing to the children and assured the people that the spirits were present with the men of the tribes and were giving them strength to make sure that the crops would grow, that the rain would come at the proper time and all would be well. But such favours could of course be withheld, and there was a definite tribal custom that in case of shortage one third of the stored grain was to be kept as a last line of insurance. Thus, living in desert conditions the groups of Pueblo Indians succeeded in holding sufficient reserves of food to make sure that their social organisation and family life could continue. The reserve was always just sufficient to tide one over to the next harvest time, when there was every probability that any drought which had caused shortage would have passed by. In fact there is no record of any Pueblo town having been deserted because of the failure of its food supply.

The position of women in the Pueblos was equally as important as that of men. However, they did not hold special meetings and they did not usually dress up or wear masks. They often ground their corn in company, on flat stones called *metates*, singing as they worked; and they spun their cotton in little groups walking or sitting, exchanging views and formulating opinions. Their conclusions in fact were greatly respected, because the elderly ladies were the mothers of the people and were looked on as advisors and counsellors. Girls would spend much time making pottery, helping in the farms, looking after groups of semi-domesticated turkeys which were bred for food, and generally being useful until eventually they married a young man of the right clan and assumed woman's clothing. It was a duty of a young man, when he married, to weave a blanket–the men were the weavers in this society–to give to his wife so that when she was first seen as a married woman she was also seen to be fully clothed–unmarried girls went virtually naked. Women's hair-dress varied a great deal, and one could tell a girl's approximate age and social position by the way she did her hair and by what kind of flowers she wore.

Among these Pueblo Indians we are entering the world of civilization–a point where a highly organized society could protect itself against its foes and hold its own in the desperate world of nature. This is the beginning of all true civilization, of all the splendid cultures which arose among the more highly organized American Indian peoples to the south.

A pottery bottle of the Mississippi Culture of around 1000 A.D., from Arkansas. This vessel has not been thrown on a wheel, but coiled by hand. The incised pattern has been cut with a sharp bone or stone point after firing. The meaning of the well balanced design is not known, but it may represent the painting on a warrior's shield.

43

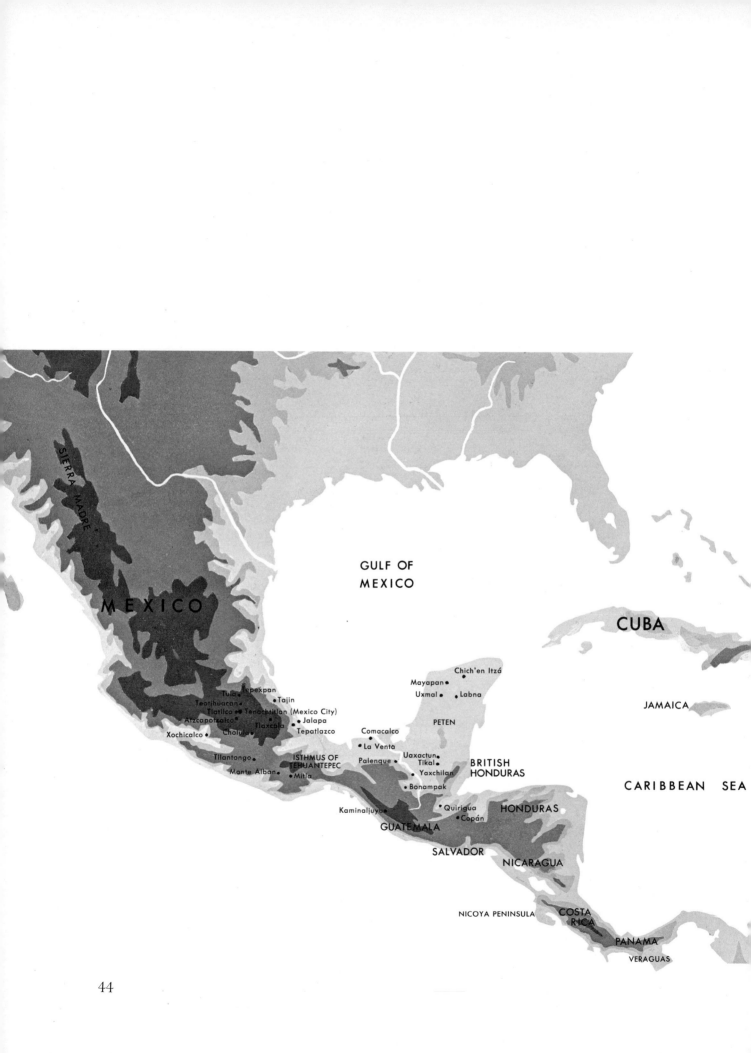

SIERRA MADRE

GULF OF
MEXICO

CUBA

MEXICO

JAMAICA

Chich'en Itzá
Mayapan
Uxmal • • Labna

Tepexpan
Tula • • Tajin
Teotihuacan • PETEN
Tlatilco • • Tenochtitlan (Mexico City)
Atzcapotzalco • • Jalapa
Xochicalco • Cholula • Tlaxcala
Tepatlazco
Comacalco
La Venta
Uaxactun
Tilantongo • Palenque • Tikal
Monte Alban • • Mitla ISTHMUS OF
TEHUANTEPEC
Yaxchilan
BRITISH
HONDURAS

CARIBBEAN   SEA

Bonampak

Kaminaljuyu • Quirigua
• Copán
HONDURAS

GUATEMALA

SALVADOR
NICARAGUA

NICOYA PENINSULA
COSTA
RICA

PANAMA

VERAGUAS

44

The Beginnings of Mexico

Although the story of developing civilization among the American Indians continues from the level of the Pueblo towns to the city states of pre-Columbian Mexico, it is best to consider Mexican civilization by commencing once more at the cultural stage of the primitive tribes of Stone Age hunters.

The history of human habitation in Mexico goes back for more than 40,000 years. In May 1967 it was announced that a site in north-west Mexico, where stone implements, human bones and charcoal had been found, gave radio-carbon and fluorine datings which show that at least 40,000 years ago hunting people were already in the country.

Mexican art, as far as we know it, begins about 10 or 12,000 years ago with the carved bone head of a coyote, which was found in a mammoth-hunter site. We have no clue as to whether this little head had any religious meaning at all, but judging from other examples of primitive art it probably represented a sacred animal of some kind. These early hunting cultures had little influence on later Mexico except that they represented American Indians of the same basic physical type. The human skull found at Tepexpan in the Valley of Mexico is indistinguishable from that of modern Mexican Indians. There is no doubt that the basic American Indian racial type was present even at this date of about 9,000 years ago. This was not very long before the period when Mexico suffered a temporary climatic change. A very thin layer of dry dust, known as the *caliche*, overspreads most early archaeological sites in Mexico, and it looks as if there was a short period in which the country really was so arid that it became unsuitable for human occupation. Changes came about later, however, which improved the climate and allowed mankind to settle down again, at first as hunting people and later as simple farmers.

We have already discussed the beginnings of maize in Mexico, and have noted that the early settlements were occupied for only part of the year by the local population, who must have spent much of their time hunting, and returned to temporary huts beside their fields just for periods of sowing and reaping. At this period – some 7,000 years ago – there was a rapid change in the animal population of Mexico. All the larger animals had died out, the mastodon, the mammoth, and the American horse all disappeared from the scene, leaving no animal which could be used as a beast of burden other than the dog. Gradually the people were able to build themselves bigger and more efficient

The earliest Mexican sculpture: a coyote head carved from a spinal bone. This work comes from the period of nearly ten thousand years ago, before agriculture had been discovered. It is a Mexican palaeolithic work comparable to the cave art of western Europe of the same period.

The Beginnings of Mexico

villages, mostly because their agriculture had developed to a point where they could settle securely in one place. Advances in the cultivation of the land probably became more deliberate. Life became much more leisurely. The discovery and development of pottery helped village life to become richer and more comfortable. The villagers used chipped flint blades for knives and dart points for fighting or hunting, but these are not really of any very high technical standard. It looks as if there was little reason for specializing this type of implement. There was a much greater development in the form of polished stone axes, adzes and piercing tools.

In the highland villages, by 2,000 to 1,500 years B.C., the potters were producing very good coiled ware. This was decorated by painting and with incised ornament. These new skills allowed the potters to sculpt their vases so that in highland village sites such as Tlatilco we find quite elaborate vessels in the shape of fish, flowers, animals, and a great number of little pottery figurines representing human beings. These arts appeared at about the same time over the whole of Mexico, although in different areas there were different tribal styles. There is no need to think that there was any real cultural unity between the different farming villages. Probably the people spoke many, many languages and were economically independent. Each village would have its council of elders and a priest, and, judging from subsequent history, possibly a specialist in military tactics who was the war leader in case of need. The little pottery figurines only rarely

Stone reliefs from the sacred hill town of the Zapotecs at Monte Alban, Oaxaca. These are two of a group of very early, possibly pre-Zapotec monuments known as *Los Danzantes* (The Dancing Men). The figure on the left wears an ear-plug and a necklet. The small head in front of the mouth may be a hieroglyph for the name of the personage. The figure on the right represents an old man. The single molar at the corner of the mouth is used throughout the history of Mexican art and is the sign to suggest great age. This sculpture may possibly represent the old fire god. Whether the beard has significance is unknown, but it should be noted that some American Indians naturally grow small beards and this does not necessarily indicate any foreign connections. Several of the figures at Monte Alban have ornamental scroll work in place of the penis. The ear-plug is shown in profile thrust through the lobe of the ear. These figures are obviously influenced by Olmec art but are later in time, probably from the second to the fourth century B.C.

46

The Beginnings of Mexico

represent men. Most of them show naked girls wearing only beads on wrists, ankles and around their necks, and with most elaborate and charming head-dresses. These are probably the analogue of the corn maidens of later cultures. They are found scattered widely over Mexico. Sometimes they crop up in middens where the village rubbish, old corn cobs, broken tools and so on were thrown. But they are often found away from settlements and may have been planted in the fields to attract the corn spirits to make the maize grow.

At the moment of writing there is some dispute as to whether the early villages in central Mexico were built up of houses of adobe blocks, or with a simple wooden framework filled in with wattle and daub. Some excavations have shown marks on the sides of the trenches which indicate that blocks of clay were actually used in the same way as adobes in later times. It may be possible with modern scientific techniques to excavate with sufficient detail to show the size of the houses and the general plan of such agricultural villages.

As time went on techniques for living improved and the Mexicans were able to develop higher cultures. The first technically advanced Mexican culture of which we have knowledge appears in the southern coast of Vera Cruz and represents a civilization which has been called Olmec. Carbon 14 dating makes it reasonably clear that the Olmecs were building earthen pyramids of considerable size a short time after 1,000 B.C. Their culture seems to have come to some kind of end, perhaps migration, or perhaps destruction by enemies, at about

Stone figure of an ocelot or perhaps a jaguar, wearing a ceremonial necklet. This creature represents the terrible powers of earth, and in later myth is a guardian of the rising sun. Cotzuma-hualpan culture, from near El Baul, Guatemala. Fifth or sixth century A.D.

The Beginnings of Mexico

400 B.C. The Olmec buildings known to us are earthen mounds
made in several stages and associated with arrangements of upright
stones, huge stone heads, and in one case a carefully buried pavement
of stone of which the slabs were arranged to form gigantic masks of
jaguars. There can be little doubt that the ceremonial pavements,
burials and the mounds themselves represent an early form of religious
belief in Mexico. The gigantic stone heads vary in size from a height of
about six to eleven feet, they are apparently all male, and many of
them wear a stylized head-dress rather like the padded helmet worn
by modern motorcyclists. There are other monuments in many parts of
Mexico which represent figures with the same unusual facial features
as the great Olmec sculptures of Vera Cruz. These figures always have
high foreheads and curious thick everted lips which give them
something of a negroid appearance. However, representations of hair
are invariably straight, and occasionally one comes across a carving in
which an individual is shown wearing a beard. Since beards occur,
although only rarely, among American Indians there is no reason for
postulating any contact with bearded people from the Old World.

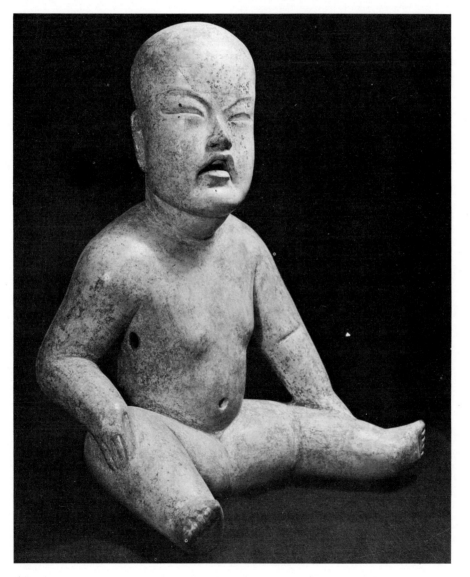

Seated figure of a child
made of coiled pottery which
has been covered with a
white clay slip before firing.
The figure belongs to a series
found in the Mexican plateau
at sites such as Tlatilco where
they appear to date from
before 1000 B.C. They
present features both of the
so-called jaguar-mouth, and
of the limbs and head form
which are characteristic of
the somewhat later cultures
of the Olmecs in Vera Cruz.

48

One of the giant stone heads from La Venta, Tabasco, now in the archaeological park at Villa Hermosa, Mexico. These huge heads were made by the Olmec people, and date from between 900 and 500 B.C. Their meaning is uncertain, but they may represent planetary spirits. None of them ever had a body. The plinth here is modern, but conceals no neck on the original. It has been said that the features are negroid, but similar features can be met with among the golden-skinned American Indian population of the region even today. Though negro navigators may have visited Brazil before the European discovery of America there is no reason to think that any African visited Mexico before the single negro soldier who was in the army of Hernando Cortes in 1519.

The great plaza of the sacred Zapotec city an a mountain top at Monte Alban, Oaxaca. The pyramids shown date from the period 400-700 A.D. though the farther one is probably a couple of centuries later. They show considerable influence from Teotihuacan in their architectural composition. Apparently Monte Alban was a national shrine of the Zapotecs, quite distinct in its Olympian character from their other sacred centre at Lyoobaa (Mitla) which was the palace of the earthly ruler and the entrance to the land of souls.

49

The Beginnings of Mexico

Olmec culture was contemporary with the revival of ancient Egyptian manners in the Saitic period but there is no reason to think that stylistic parallels between Saitic sculpture from Egypt and Olmec art represent any real cultural contact between the two far distant peoples. Many of the Olmec carvings have symbols on them which can only be a form of writing, although it is totally unlike any Egyptian hieroglyph. These symbols have a little in common with the later Zapotec and Maya styles of writing but they are never quite the same. On the whole it seems that Olmec symbols were basically meant to mark certain sacred days in the calendar, perhaps the beginnings of years. So they present a unified picture in which only a very few hieroglyphic symbols are actually displayed.

Olmec art reached very high levels. Their pottery is good, and it is worthwhile noting that some of the more ancient pottery figurines from Tlatilco are somewhat similar in style to Olmec art especially when human figures which display baby-like features are concerned. However, this rich culture of the Olmecs disappeared suddenly from history. There is no obvious reason why this should be so. It may be that these people were inspired to migrate to some other area. Be that as it may, during the years of Olmec greatness works of art in their very well-defined style were made in many regions of Mexico. They

Portico of a palace-temple at Lyoobaa, known as Mitla from the Aztec translation of the Zapotec name which means the Place of Souls. This was part of a complex of buildings from which the Uija-Tao or priest-king of the Zapotecs ruled his theo-cratic dominions. Originally the background of the relief panels was painted dark red and the patterns stood out brilliantly white. The style of architecture shows strongly the influence of Teotihua-cano design. Zapotec work of uncertain date, but still in use in the early sixteenth century.

have been found in central Mexico, north-west Mexico, and in the Zapotec country. A grey type of jadeite from Oaxaca was used for making large ceremonial axes which display the face of an Olmec deity who is always shown with everted lips like a jaguar's mouth, and with a cleft on the top of the skull. Apparently Olmec religious influence in art spread all over Mexico but we have little evidence as yet to suggest that political organization, or perhaps even an empire, had been brought to developed status at this early date in Mexico.

The great achievement of the Olmec was the use of hieroglyphic symbols. Their neighbours to the west, the Zapotecs, who lived in the state of Oaxaca were also using a system of hieroglyphic writing. Some of their early work in sculpture, in particular 'Los Danzantes' at Monte Alban, has resemblances to Olmec style. However, Zapotec glyphs which are known to give full dates, including year and day counts, are similar to but not identical with glyphs found on Olmec sculpture. It seems that the Zapotec glyph forms evolved independently although the idea almost certainly came from Olmec sources.

At Monte Alban there was a change of culture about the second century B.C. in which more definitively Zapotec art styles were evolved. From the pottery of this period it is quite clear that the Zapotecs were already particularly interested in the rain god. Vases in the form of this god with his curious serpent-like features have been found from the earliest period, but they do not become fully definitive of the type until the second century B.C., whence they continue with comparatively slight change in style right through to the sixteenth century A.D. and the Spanish conquest. The Zapotecs were a strongly independent people loving their freedom and keeping very much to themselves. Their homes were in the rich agricultural valleys of Oaxaca and their early great city stood on the sculptured hill of Monte Alban. Here they prepared an enormous courtyard levelled out of the rock. Around it they built a series of typical temple buildings which in many cases can be identified by the figures of the god or symbols carved on them. Zapotec culture was stable in the home land, spreading only gently to the south west where settlements on the Isthmus of Tehuantepec lasted until the Spanish conquest. They invaded central Mexico, but were not engaged in any struggle with the Mexicans of the high plateau until the later years of the Aztec kingdom.

In the eleventh century the Zapotecs seem to have suffered a disastrous defeat at the hands of a neighbouring mountain tribe, the Mixteca, who were powerful enough to seize Lyoobaa, the ancient Zapotec holy place, now known by its Aztec name Mitla. On the ancient Zapotec buildings here a number of fragmentary frescoes have been uncovered. They are in the style of the Mixteca and probably belong to the time of the hero of the Mixtec people, the Lord Eight Deer of Tilantongo. These Mixteca were united only for a short period during the reign of their famous chief Eight Deer Ocelot Claw. But it appears that later on after the death of Eight Deer, the Zapotecs recovered their power and drove the invaders back into the mountains. We must take it that Zapotec history is quite separate from that of the rest of the Mexican people, although from time to time their pottery styles show strong influence from whichever cultural group was ruling on the high plateau around Mexico City.

To the north of the old Olmec country there were several other tribes who flourished at the beginning of the Christian era. These

A stone *palma* of unknown use, but possibly worn tucked into the loincloth by men taking part in the sacred ball game. This beautiful sculpture of a turkey probably symbolises a god since the creature has human arms. The blue wattles all over its head suggest a representation of the Chalchiuhtotolin (Jade-jewel bird), the equivalent of the Aztec god Tezcatlipoca. Totonac work from the province of Vera Cruz, probably tenth to twelfth century A.D.

Pottery figurine representing a laughing baby boy, wearing earrings, necklace and embroidered chest band. The object in his hand may represent a fruit. This is said to be a form of the deity later worshipped by the Aztecs as Xochipilli, Flower Prince. Classic Totonac work, tenth or twelfth century A.D.

A complete section of design on the walls of the ceremonial ball-court at Tajín, Vera Cruz. The artistic style with its curious double outline is characteristic of the Totonac people. The carving represents a mythological event connected with rituals of war and the ball game. The top section represents a quetzal bird and a jaguar. The meaning of the band at the bottom of the scene is uncertain, it may represent water, or the intertwining serpents of earth. The two central figures wear crowns with scrolls in front which may indicate that they are gods. The game symbolises the struggle between sunrise and darkness.

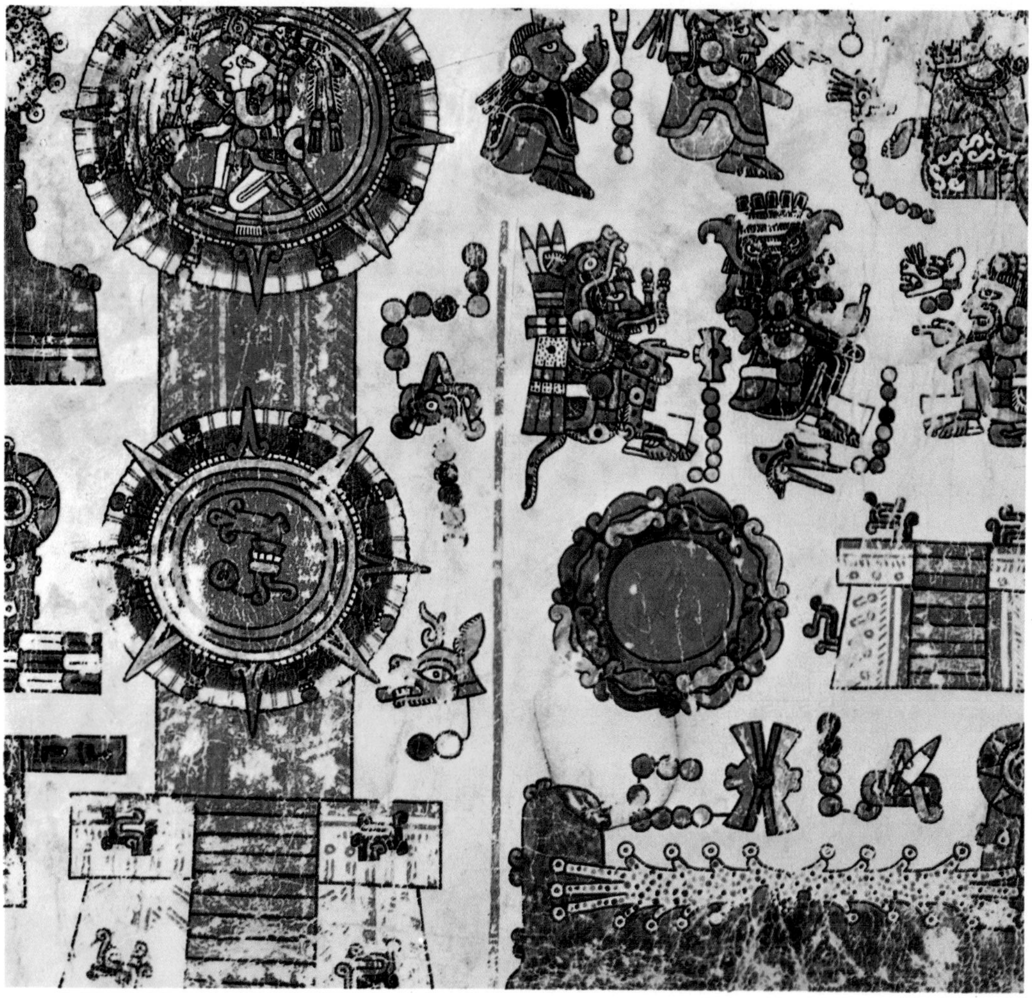

Page 30 of the Mixtec painted document *Codex Vindobonensis Mexicanus I.* This document painted on long strips of deer skin about A.D. 1350, folded into pages about eleven inches by eight inches in size, contains a short history of the Mixtec people on one side; on the other is a history of the creation and of the god Quetzalcoatl and his people the Toltecs. This codex was sent to Cortes in 1518 before the Spaniards had entered Tenochtitlan (Mexico City). It reached Europe in 1519. It was impossible to give calendar dates to the Toltec history in the codex until the figure on the left hand side of this page was interpreted, early in 1968.

This record of a solar eclipse with the planet Venus ascending towards the sun was checked against seven eclipses which had passed over Mexico in the period in which the Toltecs were thought to have been in power. Only one fitted the condition; the eclipse of 16 June 690 A.D. just after midday. Thus the whole of the Toltec history in the codex could be correctly dated.

A golden pendant excavated by Dr Alfonso Caso from Tomb No. 7 at Monte Alban, Oaxaca. Although Monte Alban was the Zapotec religious centre, this particular tomb contained a treasure of Mixtec goldwork, probably dating from the great raid upon the Zapotecs led by Eight Deer Ocelot Claw of Tilantongo in the eleventh century. Museo Arqueologico, Oaxaca.

Below:
The headdress of quetzal feathers which was presented to Cortes by Moctecuzoma as a gift for his sovereign, Charles V. Now in the Museum für Völkerkunde in Vienna, it is the only one that survives.

The Beginnings of Mexico

include the Huaxtecs, who lived on flat tropical coast lands which are now the home of the great Mexican oil industry. Because of heat and humidity these Huaxteca nearly always went naked. They built quite good houses and courts for playing a sacred ball-game which was a reflection of the moving of the stars and the sky. They were good agriculturalists, and excellent potters. In later times they were successful traders bringing tropical coast products up to the dry lands of the high plateau, where they exchanged their fruits and flowers for stone implements and jewellery.

Vera Cruz was the home of the Totonacs whose ancestors had built up a culture of their own from the tenth century B.C. They were very good workers in stone and have left a great deal of interesting carving showing that they worshipped the same system of deities as the Aztecs, though no doubt under other names. They were invaded from time to time by powerful states which arose in the Valley of Mexico, and their art is influenced by the highland traditions. However, they had a system of picture writing and built such great erections as the temple at Tajin – which contains 365 small square niches on its pyramidal faces. Apparently there was once a little image of a god for each day of the solar year on this building. These Totonacs were clever agriculturalists, they cultivated cocoa and tropical fruits. They were skilled in making jewellery from coloured shells and were also traders. Their trading canoes set out on voyages which went north to the Huaxtec country and south to the Maya lands bringing goods of all kinds. They produced very good tropical cotton in their coast land, and this was a valuable article of trade especially since they were very skilled at weaving and dyeing. They seem to have been involved in wars which in the seventh century A.D. brought some of their typical flat stone axes, carved in the form of human heads, southwards to the ruined Maya city of Palenque. The buildings in which these Totonac style stone blades were found were actually rather poor, roughly made constructions, built within the ruins of the city of an older, more splendid Maya culture.

However, the greatest innovation in Mexican culture occurred on the high plateau, a little to the north of the site of Mexico City. Here arose one of the really great cities of the world, Teotihuacan. Recent work on carbon 14 dating suggests that the greater pyramids in Teotihuacan – the Pyramids of the Sun and the Moon – were commenced about the second century B.C. when most of the highland peoples of Mexico were still living as small farming communities, making little pottery figurines of fertility goddesses. Teotihuacan started off with a great ceremonial roadway down the centre of the city site leading to the biggest pyramid in the whole of the Americas – the Pyramid of the Sun – which is 600 feet in width at the base and over 220 feet in height. It was built up in three stages, and within the heart of it there have been discovered traces of a much smaller and earlier pyramid, so the site of this great building was undoubtedly sacred even before the Teotihuacanos built their city.

Within a couple of centuries Teotihuacan had become a well planned and organized city state. In the centre was the great square which fronted the main temples. The so-called 'Street of the Dead' led from it. This avenue was flanked on either side by smaller mounds and temple pyramids built in a special architectural style which seems to have been invented at Teotihuacan. The surrounding area

Pottery figurine from the Jalapa area of Vera Cruz. This was possibly made by the ancestors of the modern Totonac people. The warrior wears his Eagle-Costume with tail and golden beak; loincloth, collar and earrings, and leg rings. The finely textured clay fires at a low temperature between 850° and 900° C. The black paint, seen on the mouth and the leg rings, is natural petroleum from oil seepages on the coast of Vera Cruz. Fifth or sixth century A.D. or possibly earlier.

54

The stele of Tepatlazco, Vera Cruz. This unusual sculpture probably dates from the seventh century A.D. – after the collapse of Teotihuacan, and before the rise of the Toltec empire. It was found at Tepatlazco not far from Tajín on the shores of the Gulf of Mexico. Its closest stylistic relationships are, however, with the monuments from the Santa Lucia Cotzumahualpa region on the Pacific coast of Guatemala. This art style developed among the Pipiles who used the Toltec calendrical system, and penetrated the Isthmus area of Mexico and northwards to Xochicalco. It may represent the art of the 'Nonoalcans' who formed part of the Toltec confederation. The scene represents an official of some importance securing the hip pad of a nobleman about to take part in the sacred ball game. Note that the player, who must use his hips, not his hands, for striking the ball, wears a protective arm pad, a knee cap, and protective bandaging round his ribs. It was not unknown for players to be killed by the impact of a solid rubber ball of seven or eight inches in diameter. Both figures wear beards. That on the ball player may be a false one to represent a star god, but the official appears to wear both beard and natural moustache. It is to be noted that most of the bearded figures in older Mexican art are found in Olmec and Totonac material, near the Gulf Coast. They may represent some tradition, or even a physical inheritance from a few drift voyagers from the old world.

A scene from one of the finest of all known Maya vase paintings. It may depict a seasonal ceremony, since the hieroglyphs at the left-hand side have the moon at the top and the sun below with a simply expressed date between them. It cannot be used for giving an actual year, since the inscriptions beside the figure are not deciphered and they may simply give the names and rank of the personages concerned. At each end of the picture are priestly attendants similarly dressed except for the waist band, which is decorated in black for the figure on the right. Both wear jade pendants on their necklace. On the raised dais a figure of similar rank is taking a jade pendant from a basket. The remaining two figures are of greater social importance and have significant additions to the standard head-dress, the pouffe of raw cotton. The one in the centre has a sacred symbol known from many Maya temples, of a fish nibbling a water-lily bud, and in front of him is a basket filled with stone tubular beads, perhaps made into necklaces. He extends a hand in a gesture of acceptance toward his visiting subordinate, who wears a quetzal plume in his headdress, and offers a red spondylus shell of the type used by the Maya as jewel-boxes. It is interesting to note that the important personages have the upper part of their bodies painted red. From the Nebaj vase, Maya classic period, probably eighth century A.D. British Museum.

An Aztec sculpture representing the god Xochipilli (Flower Prince). His tassel of hair shows his youth, and his fine jewellery defines his quality. Leg and arm rings with golden bells are worn with a nose pin, and a helmet in the form of the head of the precious quetzal bird. The god represents the male aspect of youth and gaiety, not an evil being but greatly distrusted by the puritan Aztecs. Fifteenth century work. Museum für Völkerkunde, Munich.

56

The Temple of the Inscriptions at Palenque, one of the great Maya cities. The temple was built about the sixth century A.D. and there is a crypt below ground-level which was used as a mausoleum. The entrance to the mausoleum was concealed by the temple floor, suggesting that the temple was actually built over the tombs of some great princes or dignitaries.

was filled with streets set out in a properly squared town plan. Nearest to the temple precincts there are foundation remains of quite large buildings – presumably the houses of chiefs and priests. Farther out there are regions which seem to have been the quarters of artisans, since one finds numbers of pottery vessels in one area, numbers of stone implements in another. It seems there was an almost sedentary town population of technicians. Farther still there are areas where one finds small mounds which served as house foundations. These were probably the homes of the peasantry on whom the whole of the rest of the social structure of Teotihuacan must have depended for food.

In fact, in the second century A.D. Teotihuacan could have been compared in size with Rome, it may have been bigger, although architecturally it was far less advanced. Remains of stone and adobe buildings show that the better houses were built on low platforms and consisted of a cluster of rooms entered by corridors and passages, but these were single-storey constructions and every opening was covered by a simple lintel-and-post structure. In the whole city there is no trace of any true arch. However, what the city lacked in variety of shape it made up for in brilliance of colouring, in the inner sections of the town at least. Areas have been uncovered which appear to have been priests' quarters and in them every single building is covered with frescoes of gods and sacred animals, symbols of the stars and of the rain, all painted in brilliant earth colours. The style of painting is very formalized and flat, but the design is magnificently alive. One can see these strange artistic creations as if they were in active movement, although almost every head is shown in profile and the feet are turned sideways to show the direction of movement much as in Egyptian art. The style, however, is totally characteristic of Teotihuacan and nowhere else. This same style appears in the decoration of painted pottery vases, which were covered with a lime plaster and then frescoed in brilliant colour.

It appears that this great city of Teotihuacan was not only a religious centre, but also exerted some kind of control over other places. To the south of Cholula the Teotihuacanos built another enormous mound and temple which was later famed as the home of the god of the Breath of Life, Quetzalcoatl. In Guatemala, at the site of Kaminaljuyu, so much pottery has been found in Teotihuacano style that it appears to have been a colonial centre from which Teotihuacano influence spread far and wide, even deeply into the southern areas of the Maya region. In the opposite direction Teotihuacano pottery is found farther to the north-west than the later Aztecs ever penetrated. In the east Teotihuacano art greatly influenced both the Huaxtec and Totonac people. It appears as if this great city was a dominant power in Mexico. Who the people were that ruled from Teotihuacan we do not know. It is faintly possible that they were the Xicalanca who are mentioned in later Aztec legends as one of the early races in conflict with the coastal Olmec people. But a name in a legend without identifying details cannot be considered any kind of scientific proof.

The end of Teotihuacan came with great violence, the city itself seems to have been abandoned, many buildings were smashed down until some of the walls were only two or three feet above the ground; they were filled up with the rubble from the structure above. In many cases it is clear that the buildings were burnt. However, the great holy

Above:
Stairway and entablatures of the so-called Temple of Quetzalcoatl, with masks of wind serpents and rain serpents forming the major decoration. First century B.C. or perhaps A.D. from Teotihuacan.

Right:
The sacred city of Teotihuacan (the name is Aztec and means The Gods Were Made Here). The view is taken from the Pyramid of the Moon looking along the 'Street of the Dead'. On the left is the gigantic Pyramid of the Sun, and beyond it the courtyard of the Temple of the Wind and Rain. This area is now known to be only the heart of an enormous city of which house foundations and precincts spread over several square miles. From the second century B.C. to the sixth century A.D.

A Yucatec Maya building, the ceremonial archway at one end of a processional road at Labna, in Yucatan. The structure of the corbelled arch with its capstone is well shown here. The geometric motifs, made by using carved blocks of limestone almost like a mosaic, appear to represent masks of Chac, the rain god. Eleventh or twelfth century A.D.

The Temple of the Warriors, at Chich'en Itzá. This is a fine example of Toltec architecture in the Maya area and dates from the twelfth century A.D. This chamber for the worship of the gods is on a pyramidal base and was originally roofed with timber and thatch. The lintel across the doorway was of wood and rested on the upraised tails of the rattlesnakes. It will be noticed that the serpents have jaguar ears, a reference to one of the military orders of the Toltecs. The walls of the building are decorated with masks of the Maya rain-god Chac, but the figure in front, the chac-mool, is the exact analogue of the Mexican Tlaloque or rain-cloud spirit.

60

The image of the plumed serpent, Toltec-Maya style, from the top of the Temple of the Warriors. The figure above is a standard-bearer.

A religious fresco from Teotihuacan. It depicts the god later known as Tepeyollotl as a jaguar carrying a warrior's shield and a feather-decorated rattle. He approaches his temple on the left along the pathway of the sky – a road marked by star eyes. The temple is decorated with a feathered crest; rows of shields hang above the doorway, and form the edges of the fresco. Around the doorway and on the crenellations of the temple there are large areas covered in jaguar skin. The background patterns appear to mean storm clouds over the mountains. A later legend describes Tepeyollotl as the great jaguar whose roaring is heard at sunrise. Teotihuacan Classic period, probably third or fourth century A.D.

place, the Pyramid of the Sun, was the scene of worship and sacrifice right up to the time the Spaniards arrived in Mexico. After the catastrophe Teotihuacano culture continued at Azcapotzalco where a smallish town was built in which religious buildings were erected. A great deal of fine pottery and figurines were made, all developed from the style of Teotihuacan. But gradually the art of Azcapotzalco faded out. One does not know what power it was that destroyed Teotihuacan and later subverted Azcapotzalco. It may have been one of the cultures from between the Zapotec lands and the plateaus. Perhaps there were warriors coming from the south who were involved in what has been recently identified as the Nuiñe culture.

This period of the sixth and seventh centuries A.D. was one of considerable movement of population. From the Pacific coast of Guatemala a people who were using what was later to be the Aztec calendrical system, were moving into the Isthmus of Tehuantepec and then onto the highlands just south of the Valley of Mexico, where they were responsible for building a temple to the planet Venus at Xochicalco, the House of Flowers. This has a date carved on it which shows an observation of the planet Venus in an inferior conjunction in the sixth century A.D. In part it fills the historical gap between the fall of Teotihuacano culture and the rise of the Toltec empire in the Mexican plateau.

The Toltec capital was built about ten or twelve miles north of Teotihuacan at the site known now as Tula but then called Tollan, the Place of Reeds. This name indicates that the builders of the town thought of it as being part of the marsh of creation from which mankind came up out of the waters.

The rise of the Toltec state is not very clearly documented; there are several later Mexican traditions, some of them written down after the Spanish conquest, but they seem to be very abbreviated and often distorted into folk-lore forms which appear more related to mythology than history.

However, there is one pre-Columbian document, the *Codex Vindobonensis* which although only of the mid-fourteenth century A.D., gives a list of the nine Toltec high-chiefs and has pictorial symbols showing the extent of their dominion. From this carefully dated record one can compare other documents and arrive at a system of dating. This is based with precision on a record of a solar eclipse which is linked with the death of the first Toltec king Quetzalcoatl I, Lord of Tollan. This event happened on 16 July in the year 790. The records

62

show that only two of the nine Toltec high chiefs lived through their
reign without war with neighbouring peoples. By the time of the ninth
chief, who was named Topiltzin Quetzalcoatl, the Toltec empire
embraced about the same area as the later Aztec empire at the time of
the arrival of the Spaniards in 1518. This great empire was based on a
military organization dedicated to the war gods, especially to a terrible
deity known as Tezcatlipoca who was thought to have lost one of his
feet when he dragged the earth out of the primeval waters. He was
an evil god on the surface of things – the Trickster, known to students of
all primitive religions. Psychologically he represents the shadow side
of the human personality. However, he was regarded also as a Sun
God and the patron of warrior orders and it was under his direction
rather than the beneficial Lord of the Breath of Life – Quetzalcoatl –
that the Toltec armies built up a great military empire.

We assume that among the many gods of their religion the Toltecs
reverenced a basic duality. They recognized the divine form of
Quetzalcoatl who was at the same time a god, the spirit of the planet
Venus, Lord of the Breath of Life and God of the Winds; in contradis-
tinction to Tezcatlipoca whose powers were mainly anti-life. Above all
the gods there was a divine duality, Ometecuhtli, who represented the
male and female creative powers of nature. This deity was so holy that
he had no temples on earth and was thought of as actually being outside
of the material universe, although penetrating it at all direction,
since every hearth fire in every house was a symbol of his existence.

The growth and development of Toltec social organization
impressed its stamp on all later Mexican cultures. After the Empire
had perished its memory was still powerful. All the later tribes of
Mexico hoped that one day they would be able to emulate the
wondrous powers of the Toltecs under their great chief, the god-king
Quetzalcoatl. The story goes that in his days maize grew so big that a
single ear of it was as much as a man could carry in his arms; cotton
grew in all different colours so that weavers had no trouble in dyeing
their material; and the priests understood the language of the birds.
Everything was beautiful and glorious and the Great Chief had nine
palaces, each one built from different jewels. Such was the glorious
legend of the Toltec city which was destroyed suddenly, about 990 A.D.

The cause of the final destruction of Tollan was civil war. The
last high chief had a son, Huemac, who fell in love with a girl of the
people and not a child of the Toltec nobles descended from the first
Quetzalcoatl. He intended to place her son on the throne, but the
nobles revolted and the different tribal nationalities among them
combined to attack the palace at Tollan. In the ensuing fight the town
was set on fire and totally destroyed. The Toltec chief and his followers
escaped to the coast of Vera Cruz and, travelling across part of the
Gulf of Mexico, landed in Yucatan where they made thir way to a
small Maya city which they made into a new Tollan. In later days
this ruined city was known as Chich'en Itzá. We shall hear more
about it when we come to deal with Maya history. The civil war in
Mexico had been so desperate that it is said that there were insufficient
people left to plant maize, and so many dead bodies were left lying
around after the battles that the country was ravaged by terrible
pestilences. The population dwindled, and 300 years later there were
only twenty families of Toltec descent to be found in the whole of the
Valley of Mexico.

Pottery tripod bowl painted
in fresco. The bowl, including the applied clay heads,
was fired and then painted
with limewash. The design
shows Tepeyollotl the earth
jaguar. Patterns beside the
face represent his claws. The
headdress has been painted
with green since the feathers
of the green trogon, the
quetzal bird, were symbols of
divinity. The outlines of the
painted areas were scratched
in the lime to prevent the
water colour paint spreading,
as well as to make the design
quite clear. From Teotihuacan, about second or third
century A.D.

A potter from Guanajuato state in the central plain of Mexico. He is a member of the Otomí tribe, who are living now much as they did in the centuries before the Spaniards arrived. The great earthenware jars are used as water coolers in almost every household in the region.

The face of the pyramid temple in the Maya city of Uxmal, called 'The Temple of the Sorcerers'.

The Beginnings of Mexico

After the fall of Tollan the various Mexican tribal groups assumed independence, each city forming a state sufficient to itself. Gradually, as their power increased, these city states fought each other. Occasionally small empires were formed in which one city would rule over two or three or perhaps even twenty or thirty other towns. The lesser towns became vassals of the victors and were forced to yield much of their crops, their weaving and many of their young people as tribute to the victorious tribes. This kind of thing bred a totally unstable culture. At the first opportunity subject towns would kill the garrison that was controlling them and seize their independence. In the ensuing battles it often occurred that a town would win its independence and go on to defeat its former conqueror.

In the twelfth and thirteenth centuries the dominating power in Central Mexico seems to have been the Tepaneca who ruled from Colhuacan, a town to the north of the Lake of Mexico. In one of their wars they enslaved a small wandering tribe whom we know as the Aztecs. These people had a tribal god whose name was Huitzilopochtli, who in later days was identified with the Toltec god Tezcatlipoca – but in any case he was a war god and regarded as the patron of brave young men.

For two or three generations the Aztecs, who were few in numbers and very poor in material things, were dominated by their Tepanec rulers. The Tepanecs planned an assault on a neighbouring people and ordered the Aztecs to take up arms to help them. The Aztecs marched out and attacked the enemy; but instead of bringing in the captives to be offered to the gods – the usual purpose of such raids – they killed every one and cut off their ears. They then returned to the city of Colhuacan without any prisoners. In front of the great Tepanec chief they were called out as disgraceful cowards who had brought no enemy warriors for sacrifice. Silently each Aztec leader stepped forward, each with a pack on his back and then suddenly over the feet of the Tepanec chief Coxcoxtli they poured a torrent of human ears, which they had cut off the slain enemies.

The chief was so horrified at this show of savage ferocity and unwillingness to honour his gods that he dismissed the Aztecs, and gave them a swampy islet in the lake as a place where they were to live apart from the other tribes of his dominion. They made their way there, and when they landed found a stream of red and blue coloured waters running down to the lake. This fitted in with the prophecy which the god Huitzilopochtli had made to them when they first set out on their wanderings nearly a century before. They followed the stream through the islet until they came to a pile of rocks, and there was a cactus plant. Sitting on top of the cactus was a beautiful white eagle – the symbol of their god Huitzilopochtli himself. They knew then that the prophecy had come true, that they had reached the place from which they would grow powerful, and under the leadership of their war god they would dominate the whole of Mexico. The first hut they built was a temple to the god, a little structure with reed walls put up on top of an earth mound. Two centuries later it was an enormous stone-faced pyramid where hundreds of captives were sacrificed every year to the greater glory of the gods.

However, it was a long time before the Aztec chiefs, by clever intrigue between surrounding tribes, managed to get control of all the region around the lake. It was not until the sixth of their chiefs was

Basalt columns which once formed an entrance colonnade to the House of the Frog, the temple to Mother Earth at Tollan (Tula, state of Hidalgo) the capital city of the Toltecs from about 750 to 990 A.D. The standing warrior figures wore helmets of white shell, and their breastplates were of turquoise colour representing the Fire-butterfly. The square columns in the background were once part of the temple building and represent warrior deities of the Toltecs with their symbols. The standing colossi have been re-erected on top of the pyramid for dramatic effect in recent times. Tula, about ninth or tenth centuries A.D.

reigning that this was achieved, by means of a great treaty with two other towns across the lake, forming an alliance to exploit the whole of the valley for the benefit of the three cities. The Aztec leaders also went to great trouble to legitimise themselves. They sought far and wide to find a princess of true Toltec descent so that their chief should marry her, and then her son would be a descendent of Quetzalcoatl. All the tribes of Mexico, after the Toltecs had ruled, considered it essential for a ruler to have divine blessings through descent from the great Quetzalcoatls of the Toltecs, who were believed to have descended from the god Quetzalcoatl himself; there was no other way in which the right to rule could be handed down. Thus, there was great competition among the nations for the hands of any eligible princess from the twenty Toltec families who had survived in Mexico.

Another very interesting group of people in western Mexico who had been part of the Toltec empire were the Mixteca or Cloud People, so called because their homes were up in the high mountains and were often covered by mist from floating clouds. These Mixteca had considerable artistic ability; they had been great craftsmen in Toltec times, working in gold, turquoise and jade, and became internationally

The Beginnings of Mexico

famous as painters of books. These documents, made of fine deer skin contained accounts of genealogies, history and also of the rituals of the worship of the gods. It happened that after the fall of Tollan one Mixtec chief, the Lord Eight Deer Ocelot Claw, Lord of Tilantongo, succeeded in gaining control of all the Mixtec villages and leading a great war in which the Mixteca defeated the Zapotec nation. However, this period of Mixtec glory ended with the voluntary death by sacrifice of Eight Deer on his fifty-second birthday.

After that the Mixtecs, retaining all their brilliant skill as artists and craftsmen, continued to live until late Aztec times in a state of independence in which each village considered itself free of all its neighbours and an independent community. There were three confederations of villages but this was more a division according to dialect than any strong political confederation. It was probably the roughness of their homeland and their reputation as brave warriors which allowed them to live in peace in such small political units. Their history is best preserved of all Mexican records because many of their painted books escaped destruction at the time of the Spanish conquest and so for a little while they were preserved in safety; sometimes being produced as evidence of ownership of land and the rights of chiefly families before the Spanish courts in Mexico City. Some were carefully preserved in the state archives and a few were sent to Europe where they have been preserved to our day.

The most important of Mixtec manuscripts appears to have been captured by the Aztecs and preserved because it contained a history of the Toltecs, particularly of the god Quetzalcoatl. This document was among the first which the Aztecs sent to the Spanish invaders in 1518 and it was actually sent to the Emperor Charles V in Austria before Mexico City had fallen to the Spanish army of Hernando Cortez. It is this book, now preserved in Vienna, which has recently been read sufficiently to give us the outline of Toltec history which has been mentioned before. It can be exactly dated only because of a solar eclipse giving the dating of the events on the Toltec side.

The Mexican painted books were joined leaf by leaf, so they were read from side to side and folded up in concertina fashion. The sequence could be continued on the other side – or an entirely new one begun. On the other side of the *Codex Vindobonensis* there is a shortened history of Mixtec high chiefs, particularly those of the town of Tilantongo, which continues until the fourteenth century, and then hurriedly concluded as if there was some great urgency which forced the scribe, instead of painting details of people, to give only names and dates of the succession of chiefs. Even these end suddenly about 1350. This gives us a date for the finishing of the codex, and proves that its double history, both of the Toltecs and Mixtecs, was complete a century and a half before Mexico fell to the Spanish invaders. Thus, this Mixtec book has become one of our most important records of pre-Columbian religious and historical matters to survive.

The Mixtec passion for keeping family records painted on deer skin has given us an unusually clear insight into their social life and into details of their history which are becoming clearer as, little by little, we discover the meaning of the symbols which they used for place names. Already at least four towns have been fully identified, and we know the histories of their chiefly families and their intermarriages. In one group, who are recorded in *Codex Egerton* 2895, we find that more

A rain cloud in stone. This carving in andesite represents one of the Tlaloques or rain spirits who float in the shape of thunder clouds and occasionally discharge their bowls of rain upon the people and fields below. Such figures of the rain-spirits were present in every temple to the rain god, Tlaloc. Bullock Collection, 1825, now in the British Museum.

Stone figure with the wrinkled face and projecting tooth of Ueueteotl, the Old Old God, a form of the Lord of Fire, Xiuhtecuhtli. The headdress of the god is not a hat, but a bowl in which fire was kindled in the temples. This deity was thought to be the pivot of the universe, linking the fire in the centre of the house with the Pole Star in the sky. He was conceived of as the earthly form of the Creator. From Teotihuacan, first century A.D. or possibly earlier.

Relief sculpture showing the birth of Huitzilopochtli, tribal deity of the Aztecs. From the precious flower-jewel womb of Mother Earth (note her claws and eyes at the edges of the block of stone) was born a son. Her other children, the stars, seeing she was pregnant had plotted to kill her out of envy. But at the moment of birth Huitzilopochtli leapt forth and dragged them down. All were destroyed, both the northern stars and the southern. The young god is marked by his headdress which contains the circular mirror with tongues of flame and smoke, and star-dots in his black hair. In front of his forehead is the sign of the year Two Reed, which was the beginning of each cycle of fifty-two years among the Aztecs. This one was probably the final one, A.D. 1507. Sculpture from the ruins of the great temple in Tenochtitlan. Museo Nacional de Historia e Antropologia, Mexico City.

Pottery figure of the god Macuilxochitl, whose name means Five-Flower (or Flower of the Four Directions and Centre). Although a deity of festivities it is clear that he is also somewhat sinister, as the ornaments representing fire on his earrings, a war-arrow in his headdress, and a golden coil of human faeces demonstrate. Mixtec work of the fourteenth or fifteenth century.

importance is attached to the female line, but in most cases we have masculine descent, particularly in the very thorough historical document which we known as *Codex Zouche-Nuttall*. This not only includes a history of the Mixtecs from the seventh century A.D., including some pictures which probably refer to ceremonies taking place at Tollan of the Toltecs, but also has one side entirely dedicated to a full life history of Eight Deer Ocelot Claw, the famous chief of Tilantongo. This gives details of visions received by the chief when he was a very young man, of the towns that he conquered, of all the tribes of the Mixtec whom he unified, and the history of the war with the Zapotecs and the peace treaty which succeeded it.

We note many interesting social points in this document, and in one particular section in the main historical side we have the appearance of a spirit from one of the planets who came to earth to marry a Mixtec princess. This is linked with a series of eclipse dates in the eighth and early ninth centuries, while Tollan was still a functioning reality and the Mixtecs were part of the Toltec empire. Thus, in a somewhat mythical history, we still have lists of persons, and a genealogy of the Mixtec people, extending right back to the time in the seventh century when their first chief was born from a magical tree at Apoala in the Mixtec country. Other Mixtec historical records continue dynastic histories in picture writing until two generations after the Spanish conquest. So Mixtec history has now been deciphered, largely through the patient genealogical research of Doctor Alfonso Caso of the Instituto Nacional Indigenista in Mexico. Through his work Mixtec historical material is now available to scholars all over the world and little by little their customs and their own special form of the ancient Mexican religion is being made quite clear to us.

68

The Aztec Power

As we have noted before, the Aztecs were a poor people in their earlier days, slowly gaining control over the shores of the lake. Once they had established themselves on their swampy island of Tenochtitlan, they were so sure of divine protection that it never occurred to them that their power could be broken by any combination of enemies, and of course this assumption lent immense strength to their armies. Later, as the population grew and the increasing wealth of their city attracted settlers from outside, some definition of the position of the Aztec leaders was seen to be necessary.

The emergent nation was threatened at the beginning of the fifteenth century–during the reign of Moctocuzomatzin I–by a combination of hostile neighbouring cities, and many of the people felt that it would be wiser to surrender than face the total destruction which would come from military defeat. The leader of the tribe called a council of the families of the leading chiefs and warriors, and after their deliberations offered the people a choice. He could surrender the city of Tenochtitlan to its enemies–or the armies could fight and they could take the chance of victory.

The people were unwilling to accept responsibility for this proposal, so he suggested that they should abandon the old tribal democracy and give the responsibility to him and the leading families who supported him. From them alone should be chosen a cabinet of four great chiefs who would effectively rule Mexico. The people accepted the resolution, feeling that dominion of chiefs of their own people, however harsh it might be, would be preferable to subjection and perhaps slavery under other conquerors. In the end the war prospered, the Aztecs defeated their enemies and won control of more cities. The organization of Aztec government was thus completed just as the great chief Moctecuzomatzin Illhuicamina (He Who Shoots at the Stars) had originally planned for the good administration of the country.

In the future the Aztec nation was led by a Uetlatoani–or Great Speaker–because he spoke not only for the Aztecs but for all the subject tribes whom they conquered in their wars. Next to him in importance came the Tlaloc Tlamacazqui–or High Priest of the Rains. In spite of being dedicated to the Rain God this priest was the leader in all the great ceremonies and his special function was to act as the oracle of the great war god of the Aztecs, Huitzilopochtli. Next to

One of the carvings from the great porphyry circular altar dedicated by the Aztec Emperor Tizoc about A.D. 1480. At the top are stars and planets, at the bottom the jaws of earth. Tizoc is dressed as the Aztec war-god Huitzilopochtli, a form of Tezcatlipoca. This god drew the earth from the waters and hence he has only one foot, the other was snapped off by the earth as he pulled her up from the depths. His footprint in the heavens is the Great Bear. King Tizoc, on behalf of his god, siezes an enemy king by the hair as a sign of conquest. This is the king of the Zapotec people, marked by the hieroglyph of a Zapote tree. Museo Nacional de Historia e Antropologia, Mexico City.

A *quauhxicalli* from the site of the great temple in Tenochtitlan. This sacrificial vessel (the name means Vase of the Eagle) was used for receiving human hearts, probably at the dawn sacrifice. The sculpture on the cavity represents eagle-feathers with tufts of down of the kind stuck on prisoners destined for sacrifice. The ocelot was a symbolic animal of the dawn, perhaps in this case equated with the rising sun who would devour the sacrifice. Early sixteenth century.

him came a Supreme Justice who had superintendence over the Courts of Justice in the country. He was accompanied by the fourth chief who controlled commerce through his special position as Lord of the Market Place. These four great chiefs between them covered the main functions of life in the Aztec state, and their regular meeting in council made sure that the civil administration, religion, war and trade, were all carefully co-ordinated.

This unity of purpose was the more successful because the chiefs were elected from a very limited number of people. It was true that different persons held the chief office in each department of life but they were all from closely related noble families. The Uetlatoani was the leader of warriors, superintendent of all legal business, and, most important of all, a properly consecrated priest who kept the regulation fasts and had the right to make sacrifices at the temples if he so wished. A particular form of his priestly function was his duty to watch the stars, at sunset, at midnight, and at sunrise; thus becoming aware of the powers which he thought of as the great gods directing the fortunes of his people.

The last Emperor of the Aztecs, Moctecuzoma II was particularly holy in his life. He passed much time in meditation and received visions and dreams from his gods, which he interpreted according to the Aztec religion. He extended the kingdom in successful wars, so that his full name became Moctecuzomatzin Xocoyotzin, which means The Great Lord, He of the Strong Arm. He was described by his Spanish captors as being tall and strongly built, although slender, having a golden coloured skin and straight black hair, with a slight beard on his chin. He was one of the wisest and greatest men known to us from Aztec history. Throughout his reign he was tormented by his knowledge that the fate of the Aztecs was likely to be determined by the return of the god Quetzalcoatl, in a year which the prophecies made it quite clear would fall in 1518 in our calendar. This event would prove fatal for the Aztecs, because it was their own patron god who had driven Quetzalcoatl away from Mexico in the first place. The return of Quetzalcoatl would signify the displacement of Huitzilopochtli and the breakdown of the power of his chosen people. The accumulation of magical signs, and curious rumours of strange white creatures riding in enormous canoes with wings like birds, produced dreams which were later told to the Spaniards.

One can have little doubt that Moctecuzoma had heard reports of the first Spanish voyages to the West Indies where Columbus had visited first in 1492 and where in the lifetime of Moctecuzoma numbers of the strange, bearded, white-skinned men had already settled. It was certain that the Aztecs must in the end identify the strangers from the western ocean as accompanying the returning God of the Morning Star. Thus fate and the Aztec system of astrology determined the outcome of history.

The Aztec people had always paid great attention to their magical books and regulated their lives very carefully to fit in with the luck both good and bad associated with each particular day as it passed on its course through time. Everybody was named after his or her birthday, and to this birth name was added a personal nick-name approved by the family. For instance, if a girl was born on the day Three Monkey it was considered to be a sign that she would be gay and love beautiful things, and singing and dancing. People were rather suspicious of such a character because of the general puritanical cast of mind of the Aztec nation; however, to make sure that this disposition would be directed into good channels she might be nicknamed lady Precious Jewel or perhaps even Lady Who Wears No Sandals. This would be a hint that she would become a very rich lady who need not go to the market place. Boys were usually given much more martial pet-names, they were called War Shield Bearer, The One Who Throws War Darts, or He Who is Like an Ocelot.

But the real name, the thing that counted, was the name of the birthday. The fortune of that day determined the pattern of life, and the local fortune teller would always be able to warn people whether their birthday was clashing with the luck of the present day as it happened to pass, or whether the luck of their birthday would be reinforced and helped by the magical date of the present day. This was immensely complicated, but the system exerted such a great influence that half of the existing religious books deal with the matter of permutation and combination of the symbols of the count of fate, or Tonalpouhalli as it was called. This count consisted of 260 days and not 365, so that any day in the Tonalpouhalli never fell in quite the same position in the solar year, until a complete calendrical round of fifty two years had been completed, and thus brought the solar year and magical time circuit together again.

Among the Aztecs the year Two Reed was the first year of their

A figure of solid jade, ten inches high, with a scarlet coral tongue, representing the god Xolotl, lord of Venus as Evening Star and twin brother of Quetzalcoatl who was Morning Star. Xolotl was feared since when he was visible he pushed the sun down out of the sky in the West. He is therefore shown as a skeleton creature from the Land of the Dead. On his back is the quetzal-feathered serpent, at once a symbol of the green earth and of the Precious Twin, Quetzalcoatl. Here, beneath the earth, below the closed jaws of the death god, the sun awaits his rising when the new day will dawn. To the Aztecs Xolotl was frightening but neither good nor evil; it was his function in nature to be the evening star and to perform his little triumph of pushing down the sun during his period of visibility in the evening sky. Aztec work, early sixteenth century.

71

The Aztec Power

The Making of New Fire. At Star Hill, near Tenochtitlan (Mexico City) a victim was slain by excision of the heart. On the breast the priests made fire by twirling fire-sticks on a piece of soft wood. In front of the victim a priest waits with a torch to light the new fires. From a drawing in the *History of the Things of New Spain*.

Right:
An illustration from the Aztec Calendar of Fate, known to us as the *Codex Borbonicus*. After A.D. 1520. This page deals with a period of twenty days which are ruled by the witch goddess Tlazolteotl. She is shown as a spirit of the moon and of suffering. She wears the skin of a sacrificial victim and her hair is shrouded by the witch-symbol of raw cotton. Her mouth is covered by the magical bird of starry darkness. She gives birth to herself, as the old moon is ever the mother of the new. She is faced by an equally terrible creature, the god of pride and warfare Tezcatlipoca dressed as the jewelled-turkey. The surrounding symbols are of suffering; the Young Prince and the planet Mercury (Pilzintecuhtli) walks towards the dark of the moon and the scorpion and serpent tell of sad poverty; the symbols at the bottom of the picture are all of darkness and sacrifice. One should look on this goddess as akin to the Greek Hecate.

ceremonial count of time. From a day close to the spring equinox they counted their years and at the end of the fifty- two year cycle they came to a point where there was a twelve day fast. All pottery and clothing were then destroyed, paintings on the temples were defaced and women stayed hidden in their homes; men would eat no cooked food, and lived austerely on crushed maize flour and water until the time of danger was over. At the end of the Great Fast the priests from Mexico assembled near a small temple dedicated to the fire god, a few miles outside the city. Here the astronomers watched the progress of the stars until at midnight, with the passage of the right stars across the horizon, a new count of fate could be opened. A man was stretched

across the altar throne, his heart cut out and replaced by a plate of jade on which was laid a piece of wood – this wood was then drilled by the priest with his cane fire drill to make a new flame.

Immediately the flame burst forth runners carried small burning torches to every other temple in Mexico. People flocked to the temples to catch new fire and take it home to relight their own hearth fires. Women busied themselves making new pottery and children, released from their period of detention at home, escaped singing and rejoicing that a new cycle of years had commenced. One never knew but that at some time in the distant future the sun would not rise, there would be no new fire made on that night and the world would once

The Aztec Power

more be destroyed. Four times previously the earth had been destroyed by the gods because of the evil nature of its inhabitants. But in this last creation man was given reason so that he could understand the gods and worship them properly with the prescribed offerings, so that at the end of the fifty-two year cycle they would once more give life to everything they had called into being. Among the greater works of celebration was the recoating of all the temples. The old buildings were covered with new layers of stone and plaster, enlarged in size and totally redecorated, thus consecrating them anew for another fifty-two years before the next Toxiuhmolpia, or tying together of the years, came around.

After a fast on bread and water for twelve or thirteen days the New Fire is brought to an Aztec household. The hearth fire is lit, and the mother lights her cooking fire and offers incense to the gods. The family may now wear their best clothes and sit on the newly woven mat which has been prepared for the occasion. From a drawing in the *History of the Things of New Spain*.

Another illustration from the *Codex Borbonicus*, here showing the fortunes of twenty days dedicated to brave young warriors. In the darkness of the starry night one offers blood and flowers under the Pole Star, while other young men, dressed with golden wigs to represent Piltzintecuhtli, the Young Prince, climb poles for prizes. The gods watching over them are Tepeyollotl (the god of the dawn and of the warriors who creep like jaguars toward the enemy at first light), and Mictlantecuhtli, Lord of Death; the fortune of the warrior can be bravery or death. Below are the rewards, golden and turquoise pendants and offerings of fine food, including a turkey with magic mushrooms.

The basis of all ceremonial life among the Aztecs was religion, which divided the powers of nature according to the sequence of seasons, particularly with reference to the growth of the vital maize crop. The great cosmic power was the supreme god Ometecuhtli – The Dual Lord – who represented the powers of life and growth and was therefore both male and female. He it was who lived outside the universe and was unfathomable and unpredictable. His surrogate on earth was the Fire God, whose image was in every home in the simplicity of the cooking fire on the hearth. Through this manifestation of the Supreme Power mankind received warmth, light, and the ability to change the nature of foodstuffs and make them palatable. This was such a vital thing that the hearth was a kind of miniature temple in every home, although it only consisted of three stones on the floor with the burning sticks of fire between them.

The state organization of the year comprised eighteen special ceremonial occasions. Some were dedicated to the special form of the planet Venus as Morning Star, the symbol of Quetzalcoatl, the tribal god of the Toltecs from whom all Aztec noble families claimed their descent. There were also great ceremonies for the god Tezcatlipoca, for he was not only the Lord of this world but in his form as Huitzilopochtli he was the patron of all Aztec warriors. His great feast, which was known as the Bringing out of Banners, was an occasion of military parades of a splendour which can hardly be imagined in our day. Thousands of warriors in brilliantly painted war coats, wearing helmets and masks decorated with feathers, together with the great nobles and army commanders who wore feather-work cloaks glittering with the plumage of humming birds, marched in procession to the central square of Tenochtitlan. Here the palaces of the emperors faced the courtyard of the enormous temple of the war god and the rain spirits. These buildings were brilliantly painted with red, yellow, green and blue on the white plaster background. The temple itself towered nearly 200 feet into the sky with a double building at the top so that the two gods who were worshipped there had separate altars. On the steps in front, running the whole height from the top sanctuary to the ground, were stains of blood – usually fresh and red, the glorious symbol that human victims had been offered to keep the sun shining and the power of the Aztecs glorious on earth.

In the great temple enclosure were many fine buildings. These were dedicated to other gods of the Aztec pantheon. Among them were the spirits of vegetation, and Quetzalcoatl in his mystic form as the planet Venus. There was also a temple called Yopico which was dedicated to the god of the west Xipe Totec, who represented the self-sacrifice of the maize plant. Just as the golden-skinned seed of maize is buried in the ground in order to bring new life, so at the beginning of creation the god gave himself to be sacrificed; he allowed his skin to be torn off and in his suffering he gave new life to mankind, just as his symbol, the maize seed, did ever after. The victims of this god were usually killed by having their hearts removed in the usual way, and the body was then toasted on a charcoal fire so as to soften up the skin which was neatly cut off, as near as possible in one piece. These victims were usually captives taken in war and it was the duty of the captor – usually a youngish warrior – to dress in their skins and dance before the god during the spring festival. This was supposed to symbolise the sprouting of corn from the old husk, for as the young man danced on each day of the twenty-day festival so the drying skin gradually broke up into pieces and was bundled away and buried in the foundations of the Yopico temple.

There were other sacred buildings dedicated to the water goddess Chalchihuitlicue, whose name means the Precious Green Lady. Her priests used to extract forced offerings from anybody who passed within reach of their dancing places during her festivals. They were particularly attached to a stream leading out from the Great Lake of Mexico, which contained a whirlpool. Here they used to make special offerings of reeds and canes stained with their own blood. They made them into baskets which were filled with incense and cast into

Stone head of a young man, carved from hard volcanic lava. Originally this beautiful example of realistic portrait sculpture was covered with a smooth coating of lime and painted. The eyes would have been inlaid with shell. Aztec work, early sixteenth century. From the Aztec capital, Tenochtitlan, now Mexico City.

The Bimilek vase, a sacred vessel carved from jadeite. Probably used for ceremonial offerings of pulque before the gods, it is covered with mythological representations. The face on the front is probably symbolic of Chalchihuitlicue, the wife of the rain-god Tlaloc. She is shown between earth and sky, and her hair represents flowing streams ending in shells. This was one of the treasures sent from Mexico by Hernando Cortes to the Emperor Charles V. It was no doubt of great religious importance. Aztec period, probably made about 1500 A.D. Museum für Völkerkunde, Vienna.

the waters to be sucked down in the whirlpool. During the ceremonies to explain the linking of the goddess with water and rain and the giving of food, the priests imitated ducks, which live on the food provided on the surface of the waters; and they splashed about in the water, quacking wildly, and rushing from place to place. If any unfortunate bystander came near enough for them to chase and sieze he was bundled up and thrown into the water. He would consider himself lucky to escape with the loss of his property, even if he wasn't drowned during the celebration.

There were other cheerful festivals, especially the ones in which maize was first brought in from the fields. In these the girls used to bring in the first ears of wheat tied up on their backs as if they were carrying baby dolls. To emphasise their youthfulness they took off their shawls and danced with bare breasts, singing on their way from the fields to the temples. After this they pelted each other and the bystanders with handfuls of popcorn which had been painted to look like pretty coloured flowers. They wore necklaces and garlands of these artificial flowers. At some ceremonies eggshells were filled with maize flour and thrown at the crowds by the dancers; the people in the crowds retaliated, so that everybody became covered with flour and the festival was filled with laughter and happy delight that the spring season had come again, and that there would be plenty of food for everyone. So the round of the year went on, ceremonies, some gay some grim, alternating to ensure that the rhythm of nature was re-enacted constantly in the daily life of the people.

For the ordinary Aztec citizen daily life was comparatively comfortable. Most families lived in smallish one-roomed huts with the fireplace in the centre. Furniture was very simple: a low wooden bench, some boxes and baskets for suspending clothes and tools, and a simple woven mat for a bed. The cotton blankets used on the bed might also be worn in the daytime over one shoulder as the men's main article of clothing apart from a loin cloth. Within the house, or in warmer weather outside it, women would put up simple looms and weave lengths of cloth. Two short lengths and one long piece would complete the dress for women. Two short ones were joined at the corners to make a poncho-like cape, called a quechquemitl, and this was worn over a midcalf length wrap-over skirt. The younger girls sometimes wore their skirts just above the knee but this was con-sidered rather bold by the ordinary Aztec citizen. The goddess responsible for all kinds of immorality and naughtiness was supposed to dress in such a wayward style. People who worked wore sandals, but the upper-class ladies went barefoot, just to show that they never had to do heavy work which would entail them walking to the market place or working in fields. Men, of course, always wore sandals, because whether they were farmers, artisans or warriors, they needed to protect their feet on the trackways which covered Mexico. There were no roads as we know them in the whole country.

Since there were no beasts of burden and no wheeled carts the paths between towns were simply earthen tracks, wide enough for two people to pass each other when carrying loads on their backs. More space was not needed and the soft surface of well trodden earth was much more comfortable to the feet than a hard surfaced stony road. Women plaited coloured ribbons into their hair; unmarried girls wore their hair long reaching down below their shoulders at the back with

Andesite carving of the god of sprouting vegetation, Xipe Totec (The Flayed Lord). The god is shown in the skin of a sacrificed warrior. At the Spring sacrifices warriors danced in the skins of their victims, to represent the living maize plant breaking out of the husk of the buried seed. On the back this figure is marked with a symbol, Two Reed, which was the name of our year 1507.

75

The dress of Aztec girls. The little ones wear their hair short, the teen-agers have shoulder length tresses, and the married women have their hair tied up into two horns which were symbolic of their patroness the goddess Xochiquetzal (Precious Flower) who was the first mother of twins. From a drawing in the manuscript now in the Laurenziana, Florence, of the *History of the Things of New Spain* written and illustrated by the great missionary to the Aztecs, Father Bernardino de Sahagún, a generation after the conquest.

Right:
The goddess Coatlicue (Lady of Serpents) who is Mother Earth. Her terrifying visage is made from two rattlesnake heads rising from the neck of a sacrificial vase. Her necklace is made from hands and hearts, and a skull. This sculpture is a poem telling us that Mother Earth yields the good maize and all food only if one is willing to sacrifice all in labour for her favours. This terrifying monolith, eight feet in height, was once painted in brilliant colour and stood in the courtyard of the great temple at Tenochtitlan, the Aztec capital which stood on the site now occupied by Mexico City. It was probably carved when the New Fire was kindled for the last time in 1507-8.

just a simple head-band confining it, but they loved to have wreaths of flowers to decorate themselves. The married women braided their hair and made it into two plaits which were pulled up and intertwined with coloured ribbons worn across the forehead, coming back to be pinned behind the ears. It was a charming decoration, and must have made the market place a very gay sight with all these prettily coloured head-bands bobbing about on the shiny black hair of the Aztec ladies.

Women sometimes wore elaborately embroidered clothing and a great deal of jewellery but only ladies of the very highest rank wore coronets and plumes of featherwork. Men wore simple head-bands, but as they rose in military rank so their decoration, of feathers and coloured cloth, increased in importance until army leaders and high nobles wore head-dresses far more elaborate than anything the Indians of the great plains of North America wore. They were also far more colourful since a great number of tropical birds were available from which the appropriate plumage could be taken.

But only the very greatest nobles, and in particular the Ueitlatoani himself, would wear the shining green feathers of the sacred quetzal bird which showed that the dignity of the wearer was not unlike that of the gods whose images were often adorned with his beautiful plumage. The only specimen of quetzal feather headdress remaining is in the National Museum of Ethnology in Vienna where it glistens quietly in a show case, but for the sake of protection it lies quite flat. Reproductions have been made and show how brilliant and beautiful this head-dress must have been when worn upon the head of a high official in great ceremonial processions in ancient Tenochtitlan. Gold was very much worn, as necklaces, earrings and nose-rings. There were also pendants and bands of coloured leather worn as jewellery; and strings of jade beads and little plaques of turquoise were built up into elaborate collars and cuffs for the adornment of the greater nobles.

The whole of Mexican life was hierarchic, in that the ordinary people paid great respect to the more exalted social orders. The higher orders of nobles were marked by more and more elaborate costume, which was intended to show their relationship to the great powers of nature who were worshipped as the gods of Mexico. However exalted an Aztec noble family might become they were never completely separated from the powers of nature because it was recognized as the highest duty of a human being to produce food. So on great occasions the nobles cultivated a small patch of land just to show that they too were respecting the great Mother Earth and the powers of the sky. But naturally the great mass of the people were the food producers, and a certain percentage of their crops was paid to the local chiefly families. In return the chiefs were bound to fight to protect their tenants, to organize them into a kind of militia when needed, and to act as protectors of the rights of all individuals in their care.

To assist them in these duties there were groups of magistrates who knew the system of Aztec law very thoroughly. All events which took place during a trial at their court were recorded in picture writing, and minutes of evidence were carefully taken down. Such documents, painted either on strips of fine cotton cloth or on lime-washed strips of deer skin, were carefully preserved, because on them were based all the claims within the community, of rights to land and fair sharing of foodstuffs. Painted records were also kept by chiefly families showing

The Aztec Power

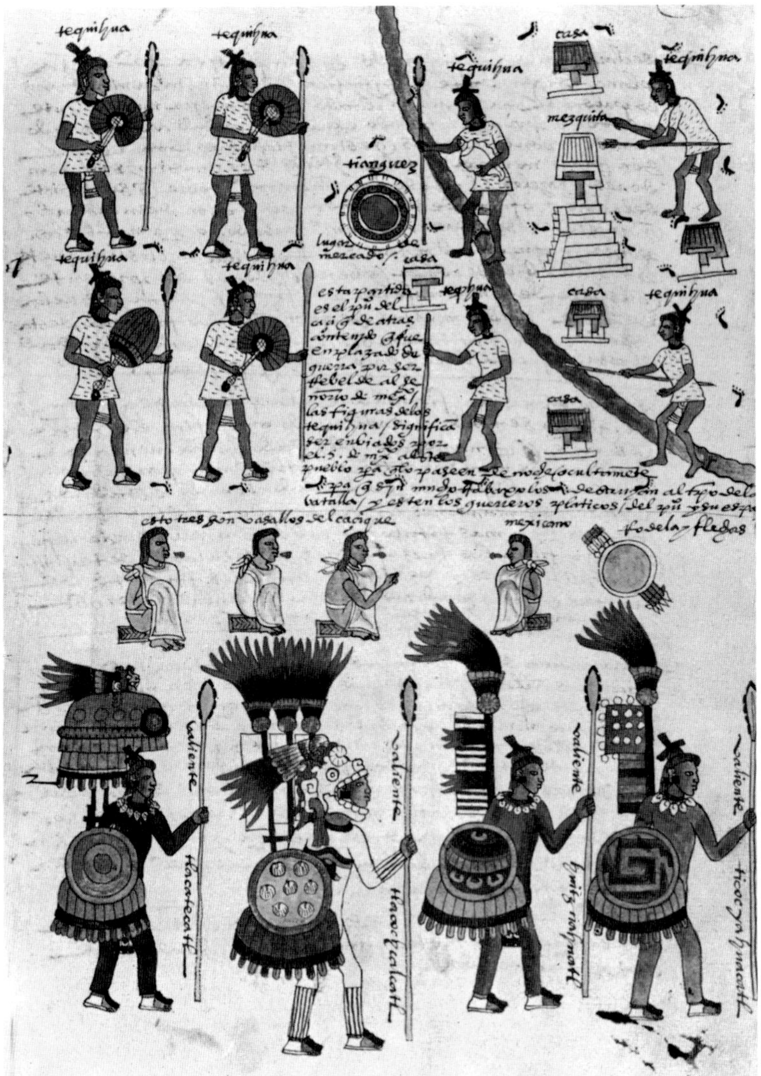

Two pages from the *Codex Mendoza*, a book prepared for the Spanish Viceroy by the Aztecs to give an account of the history of their nation, its customs, and the tribute formerly paid to the Emperor Moctecuzoma. *Below, left:* in the upper section, Mexican warriors enter a town in peace but are threatened by the local warriors. A chief receives his vassals and a discussion ends in a threat of war (the shield and arrows). Below, the great war leaders of the Aztec army in order of seniority. Each carries his shield and feather-work back ornament to show his rank. The leader carries the banner of Huitzilopochtli and the shield of Commander in Chief. *Below, right:* Aztec daily life. Top section: the two choices before a youth. Following the words of his father he either goes to the Calmecac (School of Wisdom) where he will learn the mysteries of religion and become a priest, or else he will be handed over to the master of war to train to become a brave warrior. A warrior was expected to serve about five or six years, and while a priest might also be a warrior he served the gods all his life. The choice took place when the boys were fifteen years old. Lower section; after military service was complete a young man had to marry the girl selected by his family, though it was accepted that he had a right to tell them where his preference lay. Marriages were negotiated by a woman friend of the family, and when the proper exchange of presents had been arranged the marriage broker carried in the bride like a child in a sling on her back. She is seen here accompanied by four girls carrying torches. The young couple are seated on a mat. Offerings are made to the Fire God as Lord of Life. After many hours there would be a feast, and the ceremony concluded with the good wishes of friends.

their descent from ancestors, Toltec if possible, and their relationship to the more important rulers within the state. There was no such thing as an Aztec without a family history or family connections, although often enough they fabricated great names and introduced them into their ancestry of six or seven generations before.

Aztec social organisation was a simple unity not unlike that of hunting tribes in general but adapted to civilised life in an agricultural community. Such an existence is easy to understand since the Aztecs themselves admitted that their ancestry did not lie very far back in civilized society. While it had been necessary for their leading families to marry princesses of Toltec descent in order to confirm the legality of their claims to lands in Mexico, natural supremacy was not long in asserting itself. When they had the whole country under their control, nobody thought of calling them barbarians or referring to their ancestors as Chichimeca – which means wild invading tribes who couldn't speak like 'civilized' men but would only make noises like 'chichichi'. Of course, the elders and keepers of traditions among the original communities knew of the various Chichimec invasions into Mexico, and were impressed by the bravery and sometimes the

78

The Aztec Power

wisdom shown by the chiefs of these vigorous tribes who, in their simple way, seized the cities of the ruined Toltec empire and started to build a new culture. However, the strains of genealogy become somewhat confused in the accounts since it was far more important to claim relationship with cultured Toltec ancestors than with the brave warriors who had originally come down from the northern prairies.

This curious social confusion was the cause of a good deal of the strange cruelty and harshness attributed to the Aztecs. For a people who loved flowers, feather ornaments, brilliant clothing and the pleasures of singing and dancing together, their passion for self-inflicted tortures–offering blood from their ears and tongues to the gods, and suffering long periods of ascetic self-denial for purposes of religious worship–seems quite strange. However, we must remember that similar practices were to be observed among tribes of the Plains Indians such as the Mandans late into the nineteenth century in North America. It seems that the Aztecs held a great pride in the simple ascetic puritanism of their ancestors. Adopting the rich life of the city dwellers of Mexico naturally created a sharp division within their own minds. This was explained symbolically by the learned

Pottery figure of a girl, perhaps representing the youthful aspect of a goddess. Her hands are held out in a gesture of offering, as if she were pouring out flowers or maize for the people of earth. The decorations on her belt have been lost, so we have no clue to her nature, though the jaguar claws on her ear-ornaments, and the tassels at her neck and elbows indicate some relationship to the goddess Chalchihuitlicue of later Aztec times, who was equivalent to the Spring Maiden of other nature-worshipping peoples. Tajín culture, eighth to tenth century A.D.

79

priests as a difference between the two gods Quetzalcoatl and Huitzilopochtli. So the Aztecs accepted this psychological division as a natural thing, increasing the number of human sacrifices and blood offerings made to the gods to far in excess of what was demanded by their original religion.

This excess of cruelty reached its shocking culmination in the ceremony when the great temple in Tenochtitlan was dedicated by the Uetlatoani Ahuitzotl. On this occasion the whole man-power of three mountain tribes was sacrificed, and 20,000 victims killed in a space of six days. This carnage was so great that with eight sacrificing priests working continuously it was impossible to conclude every sacrifice with the ritual cannibalism usually indulged in. A great number of bodies were thrown into the marshes to rot in the way that bodies of ordinary prostitutes were thrown away according to Aztec custom. It was this great killing which made the Aztecs particularly hated among their subject tribes, and prepared the way for the general revolt which made the Spanish conquest of Mexico so easy a generation later. However, in the regular everyday ritual the mixture of barbarism and glory was so united as to seem to the people a natural part of life.

At one time or other every young Aztec man had to take up a period of military training in which he went to a kind of special school where he was treated with great severity. The young warriors were drilled constantly in arms, and allowed no respite. They slept on hard floors, were sent on long training marches, and kept on short rations of food. In their mock battles they were issued with real arms and were given practical if uncomfortable training in the stoicism with which a true Aztec warrior should regard the cuts and bruises which befell him in combat. They were trained to look upon bravery and ferocity as their greatest glories. They were to be like the wild cat – the ocelot – seeking out the enemy in the dawn, creeping cautiously and then leaping on his foe and tearing him to pieces. Or they were trained to be like the eagle flying through the air and sweeping on the victim as if they were diving from the sun, Tonatiuh, to make captives and enrich the altars of Mexico with the sacred cactus fruit, which was their euphemism for the human heart. If possible, a warrior would capture his victim by catching him in a net, and tying him up; or else by striking the weapons out of his hands and forcing him to surrender.

Captivity, which eventually meant being sacrificed to the gods, was considered something far more honourable than being slain on the field of battle, which was a dreaded disgrace. So a warrior was prepared to surrender when in a tight corner knowing that eventually he would be well cared for until one day he would be beautifully dressed and escorted up the central pyramid. At the top he would be bent over the high, narrow stone where his breast was strained taut so that the sacrificial knife should cut quickly and easily to remove his heart. His soul flew upwards to become one of the eagles which carried the sun in his journey through the heavens. Such a death was considered glorious and entitled a warrior to be regarded by his own people as a great hero about whom songs were sung.

Apart from their strange religious and social life the Aztecs were remarkable for their technical ability. Although not conditioned in culture through a long ancestry their leaders were desirous of making Tenochtitlan a beautiful city. It certainly became one, with a population of over a million people at the time of the Spanish conquest. They

Following the Spanish conquest the Aztecs learned new ways. Here they are preparing European-type sculptures for the new Mexico City. They are, however, using the old Aztec techniques for splitting rocks with levers and sledge hammers. From a drawing in the *History of the Things of New Spain*.

imported instructors in the arts, especially Mixteca from the mountains of Oaxaca, who prided themselves on preserving Toltec traditions in art and culture. From these teachers the Aztecs learnt the art of painting books containing both history and religious instruction. They were also taught the skilled work in hard stones such as jade and turquoise which were used as jewellery. Their merchants travelled great distances, going far south into Guatemala for jade and into the Pueblo areas of New Mexico in search of the even more precious turquoise. Excavations have shown that Mexican merchants took balls of tropical rubber for trade with Pueblo Indians, presumably for this purpose of collecting turquoise for jewellery.

The caravans of merchants were conducted by members of a special guild known as the Pochteca, who were dedicated to a god of their own. They had secret rituals, and when travelling never omitted to tie their travelling staves into a bundle every evening, to which they made offerings because it was a symbol of their god. They never carried arms. Wherever they went with their long caravans of porters, carrying merchandise for exchange they were made welcome.

The travelling merchant was, in effect, the newspaper of his day. He passed on the information from all the towns he visited on route, and took back with him messages and still more recent information which he had gathered in the market places. His presence was always a delight to the townspeople because they knew that his caravan would bring them fine things which could not be made locally. From the tropics he took fine feathers and cocoa beans northwards to his home city; from the wilder northern lands he brought precious stones, arrow heads and fine animal skins; from the sea coasts he brought salt; from the mountains he brought rare timbers and fine stone for artisans to work on. Never considered among the Aztecs as a person of high social rank, the merchant yet played a special part in Aztec society. Had that civilization lasted longer he would have assumed the social importance that he held in the world of medieval Europe.

Aztec men normally spent part of every year in the fields growing food for their families, but there were also specialist craftsmen who were invited to work for the temples or for noblemen. When at work they were given regular food and shelter and often kept separated from their families. At the conclusion of a spell of work they were given valuable presents, as an appreciation of their services and a recompense for the things which they could not produce for their families while carring out their special skills. The equipment of artisans in ancient Mexico was limited by the fact that they had almost no metal. Copper was more for decoration than for any real use. A very small

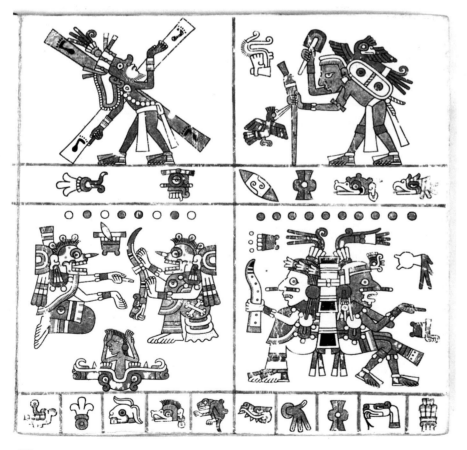

A page from a magic book, the *Codex Fejervary-Mayer*, used for prognosticating the future. The upper portion shows the bearers of fortune. On the right is the merchant carrying a pack of jade beads, and a still more valuable quetzal bird; he comes from the south – marked by the humming bird. To the left is the god of the merchants, Yacatecuhtli. He is at the crossroads of the world; with one hand he demands and with the other he offers. On the left young men die (are swallowed by the jaws of earth), and the ruling powers are the Lord and Lady of the Dead. The red serpent between them shows that the death was due to some carnal sinfulness. On the right the deities are Xochiquetzal (Lady Precious Flower) and Xochipilli (Flower Prince). They represent temporary happiness, but beside them the bowls of food are upset. Said to be Mixtec work, but more probably from southern Mexico. Early sixteenth century A.D. Original in the City of Liverpool Museum.

amount of bronze was made, mostly for use as chopper blades, but it was also worn as a kind of jewel in the form of glittering plates and little rattling bells which were attached to the borders of garments. In point of fact almost all the equipment of a Mexican technician was made of wood, bone and stone. Stones used were generally very hard. Big axes were made from diorite, and small chisels of specially hard stones – such as various forms of jade – were in use. The sharp cutting instruments were made from chert, and some arrow points and knives were made of a natural volcanic glass which we know as obsidian.

Much of the shaping of hard stone was done by strips of leather or cords which were moistened and dipped into abrasive sand – this adhered to the wet cord and produced something like an emery board. It could be used for gradually sawing blocks of stone into shape and for rubbing details into the face – both as grooves and curved surfaces. This work was slow and immensely laborious. Probably the nature of the process conditioned the great simplicity of form, which gives strength, and sometimes beauty to Aztec sculpture. However the Aztecs in Tenochtitlan itself had an immense natural supply of tezontli, a rather soft volcanic lava, which could be battered and ground into shape fairly easily. Statues were then covered with a cement-like paste, carefully smoothed and polished over so that the pores of the stone were filled and then they were painted. Thus, once upon a time the images of the gods must have looked almost like real people covered with their symbolic patterns, faces painted, and all of them dressed in elaborate clothes of fine coloured cotton and feather work.

Aztec painters not only decorated statues and painted the temple walls with bright coloured frescoes, they were also highly skilled in painting the magical books which preserve much of the beauty and directness of statement which characterized Aztec pictorial art. The whole thing was based on an elaborate code of symbols so that in these documents human figures can be analysed. Costume, face paint, postures of hands, feet, the decorations of the head-dress and the shape of the mouth all indicate status and sometimes the name and nature of action of the person depicted. In front of the mouth there are sometimes scrolls which by their colour show the nature of the speech which has been uttered. Place names were painted in a form which adds up to a rebus. That is, the names of different parts of a symbol can be put together and read as a word. For instance a stone (Tepetl) on which grows a cactus (Nochtli) is placed on a square base which shows two teeth (Tlantli). The whole of this little picture reads Tenochtitlan: from Teptl one takes the symbol *te*, from Nochtli, one takes the symbol *noch*, the base symbol with Tlantli becomes *tlan* and one adds the syllable *ti* to make titlan – 'at the place of'. Thus the picture reads 'Tenochtitlan' which means the same thing as the picture conveys, 'At the Place of the Cactus Rock'. This elaborate system of writing took much time because the drawings were very beautifully made and coloured. However, it enabled ideas to be read in many different languages, thus being of much more practical use in the multi-lingual Aztec empire than a syllabary or an alphabet.

The essential unity of each tribe seems to have depended very largely upon its own town structure. The town, with its chief and the organized officials under him, was the most important social unit. As it extended its rule over neighbouring villages and weaker towns it increased the status of its own people into that of a dominant nation,

A pottery vase from Colima state representing an edible dog. The whole vase is covered with a red-brown slip paint. Such vessels are commonly found in tombs and may have represented either a domestic pet taken to the other-world, or a supply of very tender meat for the journey. About the twelfth century A.D.

Figure of a worshipper in Aztec style. This has been carved in a soft porous lava, and is covered with a layer of much eroded stucco. The final smoothed surface can be seen on the right hand where even the finger nails have been shown. Such figures were painted in natural colours, and placed in the shrines or on the upper platforms of the temples. Fifteenth or early sixteenth century.

such as had happened in the case of the Aztecs. However, the subject people did not change their tribal identity, nor did they lose their language. Conquest by the Aztecs was just about as brutal as conquest by the ancient Assyrians. The subject people were forced to pay tribute to the limit of their ability, and failure to pay the tax collectors might mean a devastating raid on the town. The burning of the temples, the destruction of the gods, and the carrying off of nobles for sacrifice to the Aztec gods were features of such terrorism. There was no idea of bringing the people into any communal unity, or improving their situation. Thus, although the Aztecs formed a great imperial domain, they never achieved any real unity within it in the manner of the more enlightened Peruvian Incas in South America.

Aztec conquest was still in progress at the time when the Spaniards arrived in Mexico. Only twenty years earlier the Zapotecs in western Mexico had fallen before the Aztec onslaught, and the capture of the last of the Mixtec towns was even later. At the time when the Spaniards reached Mexico some of the Aztec armies were fighting in the north, moving towards the north-western area which was known to the Mexicans as the land of the Yopis, or Westerners; others were engaged in consolidating control over a wide band of territory extending into Guatemala, which had become an important centre for trade.

Within two days march of Mexico itself there was a small mountain state, Tlaxcala, which retained a stubborn independence in the face of Aztec threats. It is credibly believed that the Aztecs allowed this state to continue its independence in order to provide sactificial victims in those years when there were no official wars and therefore no prisoners for sacrifice. Expeditions were arranged with the Tlaxcalans, in which a few hundred warriors on either side competed to rope in prisoners to be taken off to the respective towns for sacrifice. This curious custom of friendly duelling was known as a War of Flowers; it was essential to keep the gods supplied with human blood so that the world should be fruitful and the sun continue to fly through the heavens every day. The sacrifice of the few victims, although perhaps terrible in our eyes, was considered by the Mexicans to be but a small price to pay for the benefit of food, light, warmth and life from the strange powers who moved in the skies, and brought wind and rain, and caused the crops to grow on Mother Earth.

The civilization of the Aztecs was brilliant in its technical ability, in its organization of the state power for the extraction of tribute, and for the great learning of its priestly astronomers and fortune tellers; yet in many ways it retained the barbarism of a tribal society. Its downfall was inevitable as soon as a more powerful adversary turned up. If it had not been for the arrival of the Spaniards it is quite possible that groups of other tribes within Mexico would have united to overthrow their hated masters. And this, as so often before in Mexican history, would have led to a period of anarchy in which many city states were competing for domination over each other. The basic premises of this kind of civilization were bound to lead to periods of breakdown and reorganization without much hope of any really great advance in civilization. The absence of the wheel and of any method of transport was certain to lead to a stagnation in culture. One can compare the people of Tenochtitlan with the Toltecs of Tula and with the race which built Teotihuacan fifteen centuries before; but one can see very little sign of cultural advancement.

The Maya People

In the thickly wooded and hilly country of the Peten, and over the border between Guatemala and Mexico, there lived in ancient times a people who were simple villagers. They tilled their fields under rather difficult tropical conditions, and produced maize as their staple food-stuff wherever it was possible to grow it. As far as we know they spoke dialects of a language which we call Maya but we do not really know what title they gave to themselves.

At the very beginning of the Christian era there came traders and possibly warriors from the more highly civilized peoples of Mexico. In particular, at Kaminaljuyu in the Guatemalan highlands, there was a very strong influence from the Mexican city of Teotihuacan. This influence was so strong that great numbers of pottery vessels and small figures were made which are indistinguishable from those manufactured at home in the Mexican city. This settlement lasted for a considerable time, probably for four or five centuries. One can have little doubt that it influenced the Maya speaking peoples in its neighbourhood. There was very good reason for the Teotihuacanos to enter the Maya country, since the Mexican plateau produced none of the things which could be obtained in this southern region. Cocoa, vanilla, and rubber from which the balls were made for a ceremonial ball game, were all of great value in Mexico and could not be produced locally. In addition the southern lands were places where birds of gorgeous plumage could be found. There were the many coloured varieties of parrot and macaw, and also most precious of all the quetzal bird which the Maya called the kukul.

For some reason, unknown to us, the Maya villages became inspired with the idea of enlargement and improvement so that early in the second century A.D. we find a sudden outburst of a number of new towns. Each of these had a ceremonial centre; that is a large courtyard which was surrounded by temples and other courtyards in which stood large carved stone monuments called stelae. The inscriptions on them recorded calendrical dates and the period in which they were erected for the good fortune of the city where they stood. No doubt there was a preliminary stage in which buildings and monuments were constructed of wood and, probably, placed on earthen mounds. It is unlikely that the Maya came from another part of the Americas with their culture fully developed. It was a unique culture and nothing really like it has ever been discovered by archaeo-

85

logists in other parts of the Central American region. It is, therefore, only reasonable to assume that it was a development from within.

It is reasonable to assume that the Maya-speaking tribes had some knowledge of the systems used by the surrounding people for recording ideas in hieroglyphic writing. It is also reasonable to assume that their particular types of buildings were basically inspired by what they had seen in the Teotihuacano settlements in the mountains and among the neighbouring Mexican tribes, such as the Zapotecs. However, it appears that the Maya were determined to produce their own type of temple, their own style of sculpture, and to use hieroplyphic writing in a way which was specially theirs. No doubt there is an echo of earlier tradition in their work, and in fact one of their earlier temples, at Uaxactun, is very like an Olmec building in many parts of its structure though it was erected some four centuries after the Olmecs themselves had ceased to make their distinctive monuments in southern Mexico.

This spirit of individuality in art and culture marks out the Maya from other Mexican people. They developed side by side with other people but in their own way. Sometimes, apparently, they engaged in military conflict with either Teotihuacanos or people from the Totonac region of southern Mexico. Their greatest advance was the full development of the ancient systems of picture writing into a syllabary. In their script they have glyphs for something like 700 different syllables. These are strung together to make words and sentences, but the system is somewhat cumbrous, and sometimes syllables are repeated with only slight variation. This is characteristic of many early developments of human phonetic writing. It occurred early in the development of Chinese ideograms, it occurs in the Minoan scripts from Crete, and something of the kind also occurs in Egyptian hieroglyphic writing. It is apparently a necessary step in the development of writing by sound, whatever the race of people in process of inventing it. After all, this is a tremendous step forward; it is not at all natural to assume that a thing seen with the eye should represent a sound. The only way in which it could arise is from drawing part of an object and then pronouncing its name. Thus, at the origin of phonetic writing, diverse people used widely diverse symbols for given sounds. However the Maya version was sufficiently good for their needs and, although it is so far still in process of decipherment, we already realize that it can convey a great deal of information.

Unfortunately, the information which has survived has only amplified calendrical symbols and is almost entirely concerned with the passage of time and the prognostications of fate after the manner of very complicated horoscopes. So far it has been impossible to find anything which seems like history and we are still bound to rely on the archaeologist's tools for our basic historical structure of the Maya civilization. There is a sequence of regular artistic developments and alterations of style; first a gradual improvement and an approach towards realism, and then a florescence which is so rich that it produces a kind of Central American baroque. This gives a rough guide to periods, and nowadays with the help of carbon 14 datings from surviving fragments of wood and bone found in Maya buildings we have an outline of dates which corresponds quite closely to the generally accepted Goodman-Thompson-Martinez correlation of the Maya calendar. Thus we are now able to read Maya dating symbols and translate them with certainty in our own calendar.

Stele K, from Quirigua in Guatemala. This ancient Maya sculpture represents a god, presumably Kukulkan, the Planet Venus as the evening star to judge by his quetzal-feather headdress, in a phase of invisibility when under the earth. The curious mask on his shield appears to represent the male form of the earth god, while the animal on the headdress is the earth goddess who has closed her jaws on the dog. Classic Maya about the sixth century A.D.

A Maya inscription of the
eighth century A.D. from a
limestone monument, known
as Stele P, at the ancient site
of Copán, Honduras. This
shows the elaborate nature
of Maya hieroglyphic writing. Roughly speaking each
pictorial element is a syllable,
and the human faces rep-
resent numerals associated
with days and months. The
hand holding a shell is one of
the forms of zero used in
Maya arithmetic. Such
columns were erected in
ceremonial centres once
every twenty years at least,
and their purpose was to
mark the changing of time
and to state the astrological
conditions prevailing.

Right:
Elaborate cornices and
relief panels on the facade of
the so called Palace of the
Governor at Uxmal, Yuca-
tan. Late Maya work of the
twelfth century A.D. The
main element of this architectural decoration com-
bines angular frets representing coiled water serpents
with masks of the 'Long
Nosed God', who is really
Chac, the Maya rain god.
The importance of rain to
the Yucatec Maya derives
from the geological structure
of northern Yucatan, which
being a limestone plateau
has no surface rivers. Hence
all life was dependent on
rainfall and natural wells
(*cenotes*).

The Maya People

There is some evidence which leads us to think that in the Peten region a group of Maya cities in the third century A.D. were united by a common version of the calendar in which they kept the count of lunar periods exactly in conformity one with another, and do not show the minor variations characteristic of earlier times. Translated into political terms which, however, must remain rather uncertain, we would think that towards the end of the third century A.D. a number of previously independent city states had joined together into a confederation. Whether this confederation was merely to bring the magical power of their religion into a unity, or whether it marked a real political unity of the kind which might be considered to be an embryo empire we cannot say. As time went on Maya culture and the ceremonial centres, with their temples, plazas, courts for playing the sacred ball game, and inscribed calendrical monuments, greatly increased both in size and richness. Some of the Maya cities, like Tikal, are not only conglomerations of temples, but contain many simple mounds extending considerable distances round the sacred centre. These appear to have been house foundations, which indicate that some cities must have harboured a considerable urban population in ancient times. Other sites have clusters of quite beautiful monuments but no evidence of local domestic settlements.

It may be that a population cultivating comparatively small plots of land here and there throughout the forest region around the city centre came together to worship the gods only on special occasions, probably once every twenty days. This would fit in excellently with the ceremonial calendars which we know were kept by the Maya priesthood. As we have said before, the whole basis of life for the Maya depended on agriculture and in particular on maize cultivation. In their forested country they were able to practise shifting cultivation with considerable success. As a clearing became leached out by the rains and lost its fertility, it could be abandoned to the forest. Trees and creepers soon grew over the plantation and constant falling leaves and decaying vegetation rapidly enriched the soil for use again in later years. New plots were cultivated by chopping down trees with stone-bladed axes and setting fire to them, so that the mixture of wood ash and vegetable humus on the ground provided a good fertile basis for a few years of cultivation.

In these circumstances the agriculturalists probably remained in comparatively small and lightly built villages. It was only with the development of the higher culture that it paid to have well-built houses raised up on mounds, for the settlement of any large section of population. Otherwise it is probable that only the houses of members of the chiefs' families were built on mounds, or prepared in any very special way.

We must look upon the Maya basically as a group of tribes, speaking similar languages, and subsisting on maize cultivation carried on in the difficult environment of the tropical forest. The whole of their art reflects forest conditions so that we find decorations composed of the growing sprouts of vines, of maize canes growing in the fields, of tropical fruit products – particularly of the cocoa tree – and, of course, a wonderful art of feather decorations derived from the many beautiful avian species which dwelt in the forests. The animals represented include deer, peccary, and occasionally a creature which seems to be the tapir which lived in that region. There were also

The central building of a great early Maya city, Palenque in Chiapas. The tower, of which the top storey is a reconstruction by the Mexican archaeologist Alberto Ruz, is the only multi-storey building in the Maya area. The main part of it consists of ranges of narrow halls with high corbelled roofs. The open space within the building is only about a third of the total space occupied. Once all walls and exposed surfaces were coated with elaborately modelled stucco richly painted. Classical Maya, seventh century A.D.

'terrible' creatures such as boa-constrictors, alligators and the jaguar, which seems to have been treated with almost religious respect. In fact they were so holy that serpent skins, alligator masks, and beautiful jaguar skins formed important parts of the costume of the great dignitaries of the Maya cities. Hunting, to judge by surviving pictures, was conducted on foot with the use of darts projected from a throwing stick, of spears and of pellet guns, in which a pellet of clay or a round stone was blown violently from a long cane tube and was capable of stunning birds. Spring traps, which caught up animals which had trodden in nooses attached to them, were in common use; and pit traps with deadfalls were used for catching dangerous creatures such as alligators. In other words, the Maya were extremely efficient in exploiting the possibilities of their natural habitat. It is most unlikely that they ever suffered any great shortages of food. Important accessories to this were their great flocks of turkeys and herds of semi-domesticated peccaries.

One can have no doubt that in a well organized village society, leisure was soon available for the construction of fine buildings and,

when the techniques reached an advanced stage, great religious
monuments. Probably the first impulse was the simple one of emulat-
ing neighbouring peoples. However, the Maya were quite
undoubtedly a nation whose cities were ruled over by a theocracy.
One finds sculptures everywhere, and occasionally paintings, which
show the priests dressed in the costumes of the gods. Those in the
enormous stone stelae stand guarding the four directions, holding a
strange double headed monster in their arms which seems to represent
the surface of the earth. From one of its heads the sun arises in the
morning, and in the other head the sun is swallowed as it goes underneath the earth in the evening. These gods of the four directions are to
be found on all the monuments and in some cases it is made perfectly
clear that the god is actually represented by the priest.

When we come to pictures of warfare we find that the great nobles
are wearing plumes of feathers, and costumes which are closely
similar to those of the priesthood. In fact, in historic times when the
later Maya were discovered by the Spaniards, it was still the rule that
the young men of great families were educated to take alternate

The Maya People

offices in the town government. For part of their lives they were priestly officials and for the other part civil administrators. They alternated from one phase to another as they moved up grade by grade to the final position when they would become either a chief sacrificing priest, or the Halach Uinic, the Ruler of Men or High Chief of a City State.

The status of the Mayan women seems to have been excellent. Of course, they were the people who ground the maize, who baked the bread, who bore babies, who wove the clothes, and were the centre of all the hard domestic routine. But we notice in representations of women that they often wear very fine clothes and very beautiful ornaments. Among the gods divine figures occur which are quite definitely feminine. In some of the pottery figurines we find great ladies represented in what must have been very smart dresses. These show variations in fashion through time, although the design seems to change very, very slowly compared to our modern concepts of fashion. They wore jade necklaces, fine earrings, and paint and tattoo designs on their faces, though they never quite indulged in the extent of self-mutilation adopted by the noblemen. They appear in paintings as members of the chief's court and obviously hold definite social position.

It is perfectly clear that among the Maya, great ladies were treated with a respect which approached that given to their husbands, the chiefs. The working women were so essential to their families that even in comparatively recent times the division of labour between men and women was always well defined in the family. It was considered wrong that a man should intrude into a woman's province to grind the corn or attempt to weave cloth, just as it was considered something really rather shocking for a woman to attempt to go on a military expedition or to go hunting. In recent times Maya custom has made the women the market experts of the family and it was probably the same in ancient times. They not only went out and sold things in the market, but they also selected and bought for the family. Thus, there was full respect paid to them as skilled traders.

Children were very much loved. At birth every child was presented with a little jade bead by its relatives as a symbol of the sacredness of life. As they grew up they received education, mostly from the family and neighbours; but every child had some special teaching in temple schools, and, of course the boys learnt discipline in military schools attached to the temples. Girls probably learnt very much more from their mothers than from the priestly teachers of poetry; deportment and the use of flowers really being of importance only to women of higher social position. The mass of the ancient Maya people had, however, some kind of education which fitted them for living a fuller life than just that of primitive farmers scratching a living from the earth.

The present day Maya still speak a developed version of the ancient language. It is rich and complex and has poetic qualities. We know that in ancient times the Maya included poetry and the composition of hymns to the gods among the specially honoured accomplishments. There was no theatre as such but at this stage of their development the religious ceremonies enacted the legends of the gods. The great plazas in the towns, surrounded by temple pyramids, became wonderfully beautiful stages every twenty days. There the priests, dressed in magnificent coloured robes and featherwork capes, danced in impersonation of the gods and showed to the people the stories behind the ritual – probably all theatrical beginnings in this world were made

Incised relief sculpture in fine-grained limestone, from the Temple of the Beau Relief at Palenque, Chiapas. This was among the earliest Maya sculptures to be published in Europe, near the end of the eighteenth century, and dates from the eighth century A.D. The central figure holds in his left hand a group of symbols tied as a kind of pendant, which seem to refer to sunset and the West. He may be a young chief, but is more probably a divine figure. He is seated on a cushion supported by two crouching figures, one of which has a tatooed face and beard and moustache. This figure faces a mask of the evening star which is the throne for a priest who offers a headdress of white shell and quetzal feathers, with a mask of the wind god on it. The other figure of the central throne faces a lizard-like mask, an earth and fertility symbol, worn by a figure which is the throne of a priestess in a fringed dress. She offers a symbol which refers to the wind god in his death aspect, of which the bottom is a symbol known as the Maya day sign Ahau (the Lord) with a jaguar-skin decoration at the mouth. These symbols suggest that the central figure, dressed as a young Maya nobleman, is regarded as the equivalent of Venus as Lord of the House of Dawn, being offered the symbols of the planet as evening and morning star.

The Maya People

in a similar way. Among the Maya the ceremonies never developed to a higher stage; at least there is no record of anything like the true dramatic performances of a secular nature which were occasionally displayed in Inca Peru.

Among the things which the Maya lacked was the potter's wheel. They used only a slow turn-table made from a block of wood which they rotated between their feet, or else a section of some large broken pottery bowl which they used to turn gently round and round as they coiled up the shape of new pottery within it. They do not appear even to have had the little wheeled toys which appear in Mexico. They had no beasts of burden whatever; we occasionally find a drawing of a dog carrying a pack on its back, but this may be more religious symbolism than real fact. There were normally only footpaths between towns; but paved roads – sometimes a few miles in length – do exist between city centres, as if for great ceremonial processions. The Maya made these causeways to allow for the proper display of the dignity and beauty of ceremonies and possibly for the conveyance of the images of the gods from one city to another. The great ceremonial courtyards were always carefully paved with stone, but in the towns built around religious centres there were no true roads, just hard-beaten earth footpaths between the buildings. There was no incentive to turn the ceremonial trackways into real roads for the transport of goods, and the comfort of porters trotting with a heavy load on their back and wearing sandals was much better assured by earthen tracks than by hard stone pavements.

A great deal of trade was carried on, by convoys of porters between the cities, and by the fleets of large canoes in the coastal towns. These were cut from ceiba or mahogany trees which could carry crews of some forty or fifty people and take bales of merchandise from one place to another. This seems to have been highly organized. In late Maya times Christopher Columbus encountered such a canoe in which the merchants commanding it sat protected from the sun under coloured cotton awnings in the centre, while rows of paddlers on either side propelled the boat towards the ports with which they intended to trade. The more ancient Maya occasionally show a canoe in a painting in one of their religious books or sometimes a canoe shape appears in sculpture, but there is no real evidence that these were very large vessels. In the painted books there are sometimes marks on these drawings as if they represented a canoe which had been made up of several pieces of wood sewn together, though this seems a rather unlikely exercise when very large tropical trees were easily available to the Maya.

We know from painting and sculpture that the war leaders of Maya towns had no sinecure. There was actual fighting of considerable violence sometimes, as can be seen from the painted frescoes of Bonampak. People were killed, prisoners were taken, tortured and slaughtered. We know that there was some conflict which depopulated the eastern Maya town of Palenque in the late seventh century, since there is nothing of a later date to be found there. Some of the buildings were occupied by people from southern Mexico who left weapons and carvings there and apparently erected simple stone shelters within the ancient ceremonial buildings. There is no evidence that the Maya reoccupied this town after its abandonment.

In ancient times there were a few smallish Maya towns in the

Life-sized head in stucco from the remains of a relief panel in a temple at Palenque, Chiapas. This represents an original invention of true portraiture, which among these people covers only a couple of centuries from about 700 A.D.

Modelled stucco head photographed where it fell from the wall of a temple at Comacalco, Tabasco. The plaited cap fringed with beads suggests that the head was in some way connected with a water cult. The unusual feature is a small beard seen in work found near the shore of the Gulf of Mexico.

The Maya People

The ball-court at Copán, Honduras. On either side of the court are the remains of important buildings, and all around one can see alignments of stelae which are time-markers. Each standing figure was one of the Bacabs, the gods who supported the four corners of the sky, and in front of each is an altar-like stone representing the Earth-Mother in her reptilian form.

The ball game was played by two teams, who bounced the ball from one to another by butting it with their hips. The aim was to keep it moving in one's own team without allowing the opposition to take it. If possible the players tried to score by bouncing the ball up the slope and through a ring at the side of the court, in this case the beak of a giant macaw head. It was a religious game, representing the movements of stars and planets in the heavens and the movements of fate. Much wealth was gambled on the results. Eighth century A.D., possibly earlier.

Yucatan peninsula. This was a difficult region because there was little surface water and the rainfall itself rapidly soaked through the limestone and ran into channels which, over thousands of years, had been dissolved out of the underlying rock. Thus Yucatan is honeycombed with underground streams and occasionally places can be found where the roof of caves have fallen in, disclosing an underground lake or stream accessible by climbing down some thirty or forty feet. This water supply was apparently only sufficient for the needs of smaller Maya cities, though life went on in much the same way as it did in the larger and richer cities of the forest country.

Some unexplained catastrophe seems to have struck the Maya of the forests at the beginning of the tenth century. Cities were abandoned, people no longer erected time stones; occasionally an earthquake cracked the front of a temple and it was not repaired, or else it was patched up only crudely. It seems as if a great part of the Maya population either died or just went away from their cities. Whether this was the result of war, of a revolt of the peasants, or of some migration under the inspiration of the gods is by no means clear. It may be that further excavation will provide us with clues, enabling us to give shape to what is at present a mysterious and obviously unhappy page of Maya history. At the same time as the abandonment of the cities of the Peten which were left to be covered by the forest, there was some setback among the cities of Yucatan, but they did not totally disappear and shortly afterwards seemed to have increased in size and influence.

In the early eleventh century the Yucatec towns were the most important ones ruled by the Maya, and here they suddenly encountered a wave of invaders coming from Mexico. These were the Toltecs whose leaders had fled Mexico after the terrible civil war which had destroyed their capital city of Tollan. There were apparently several strains of these Toltecs, the most important of which were the Xiuh clan, but there were also the Itza who seem to have reached Yucatan at some earlier period and migrated along the coast, thus isolating their Maya rivals, the Cocomes.

The invaders were groups of nobles ruling military states somewhat after the Mexican fashion. The main feature of the Toltecs' presence in Yucatan was the building, by the side of a small Maya ceremonial centre, of an enormous city. This had palaces, ball-courts and great pyramid temples in a thoroughly Mexican Toltec fashion and was built near one of these strange lakes which were like gigantic wells. This city was known to the Maya as Chich'en Itzá – or The Well Mouth of the Itzá. Here the Toltecs worshipped their Mexican gods but they appear to have been mostly a military clan using Maya labour for the construction of buildings and in the immense amount of carving and painting which decorated them. It was a city of great beauty, designed to reflect the glories of Tollan which they had been forced to abandon in Mexico. They were very careful in compelling the local people to work precisely to Toltec standards, but it is to be noted that the Maya style of building is employed throughout and there is far less use of cement than in the original home town.

From Chich'en Itzá the rulers of the Toltecs controlled many other cities. There were occasional wars, revolts, and political trickery but for nearly two centuries this beautiful Mexican city lorded it over a population which was becoming increasingly Maya in

The Maya People

nature. We find inscriptions in Maya hieroglyphs, and paintings appear in thoroughly Maya style in the later buildings. Even the names of gods are changed into Maya. Tlaloc, the Mexican Rain God, is identified with the Maya Chac and is given his name. So that even the statues of the little rain clouds who carry bowls of water in their arms are no longer known as Tlaloques, but as Chacmuls which is the Maya equivalent of the Toltec word. The Mexican deity Quetzalcoatl is given his new Maya name Kukulcan, which is a direct translation, but it implies that the head of the Toltecs at Chich'en Itzá, who was named after the god, was now given his ceremonial and sacred title in the Maya language.

This does not explain the final breakdown of Yucatec culture because what had really happened was an almost complete assimilation of local Maya and Toltec families. They seem to have spoken the same language, worshipped the same gods, and had the same system of political intrigue and warfare. Little by little, as the Toltecs became less unique in the region, other city states conspired, until finally Chich'en Itzá itself was overthrown, and a new centre of government was built in a very much poorer way at the not very distant site of Mayapan. The very name indicates the mixture, because the *Maya* part indicates the language (and it is also perhaps a racial definition) and *apan* is really the Mexican word for a chief's courtyard. The name of the city itself belongs to the two ruling groups. Here the internal struggles continued, until finally the whole of the Toltec-inspired culture in the Maya country collapsed in a series of little civil wars between city states. Among these one cannot point out any very clear leader. The real Maya centre was at Uxmal, an ancient town made more glorious in later times by its rulers the Cocom family. At Chich'en Itzá the Xiuh clan continued Toltec rule, and their leader the Tutul Xiuh was titular head over the whole of Yucatan, but this seemed to have meant as little as did the title Holy Roman Emperor given to a selected member of one or other of the German princely families in the eighteenth century. The Itzá people themselves left northern Yucatan after the fall of Chich'en Itzá and took refuge in the far southern forests where they built a town at Tayasal. They disappear

Three views of the great Toltec-Maya city of Chich'en Itzá. Centre: the pyramid temple was sacred to the plumed serpent – the god Kukulcan (the Maya name for Quetzalcoatl). Left: the sanctuary of the Temple of the Jaguars, seen in the background, is built on the wall of the Ball Court; the great serpent head in the foreground is at the approach to the Temple of the Warriors. Right: the Temple of the Warriors seen from above.

The Maya People

from the main stream of Maya history until their conflict with the Spaniards almost a century after the invaders had subdued Yucatan.

The period between the fall of the old Maya cities of the forest and the beginning of the new mixed Toltec–Maya culture was one of some intellectual development, since it is from this time that we have the two most important surviving Maya picture manuscripts. These are the *Codex Dresdensis* and the *Codex Peresianus*. The latter is particularly important, although much damaged, because it shows a series of animals descending from the heavens which can be equated with the signs of the zodiac. Since the Maya were not dividing the year quite in our way there are minor differences in the forms shown, as observed in the stars, but there are also some interesting correspondences, including a scorpion which is in exactly the same area of the zodiac as our constellation, Scorpio. The Maya had thirteen zodiacal signs, and the reason for this is much the same as for the twelve Babylonian signs. They represent the area of sky which had passed across the horizon at sunset each day during the twenty-nine day period of a moon.

On the whole the Maya were more logical than the Chaldeans, since every year contains twelve complete lunations and part of a thirteenth. This logicality is quite characteristic of Maya thought and the codices, like the more ancient stone monuments, are full of calendrical calculations. These are based on a time rhythm similar to that adopted by the peoples of Central Mexico; that is, a series of twenty named days combined with a series of thirteen numerals, thus making the magical calendar round of 260 days. The Maya, like the Aztecs, also found it advisable to use a civil year as well as the magical time count, for the very good reason that farming was only possible on the basis of a solar year. The time for planting and the time for reaping were conditioned by the position of the sun in the heavens, by the passage of rain-bearing winds across the country at definite times and by periods of comparatively great heat affecting the ripening of the maize crops. There was never any question of breaking any rhythm of time, the count of days went on continuously. Every 260 days they had a new day-beginning named One Ahau–One Lord– and that ended the count, again to be repeated in 260 days. But each

year was given its own internal count of a series of eighteen of the twenty-day festivals, plus five days at the end, just as among the more northern Mexicans who more probably learnt the system from the Maya. There was no intercalation in the Maya long-count system of time recording. They counted 360 days at a time, and the special month of five days was only counted on as part of an official year not of a time cycle. When dealing with time the Maya astronomers dealt in periods which they called stones or *tun*. These consist of 360 days precisely; the next larger time period was a Katun–twenty times 360 = 7,200 days; the next higher unit was the Baktun–twenty times, twenty times 360 = 144,000 days; and beyond it came the Pictun –twenty times, twenty times, twenty times 360 = 2,880,000 days, which was quite a long period of time to be covered in a calculation.

This, of course, did not exhaust Maya mathematics. In their inscriptions they are found to have adventured into theoretical calculations, presumably connected with their religion, which take one backwards and forwards in time for spans covering hundreds of thousands of years for which there could have been no recorded history whatever. The basis of all this calculation is straight-forwardly astronomical. The movement of the sun, moons, and planets around the earth, passing through the different groups of stars in due season, was all carefully recorded. The Maya astronomers were fully able to calculate the occurrence of solar eclipses both backwards and forwards in time, but since they were not aware of the extent or the shape of the earth they could only tell when an eclipse syzygy would occur and not necessarily whether they would observe the eclipse itself. If one looks at a map showing eclipse tracks over a period of time one will note

A vignette from the *Codex Troano-Cortesianus*, a fifteenth-century Maya manuscript painted on paper made from the inner bark of a fig tree. The scene represents four deities playing on friction drums. They are pulling on cords rubbed with resin attached to a skin membrane within the drum. The noise produced resembles the howling of a jaguar. Some authorities have described this picture as one of the gods making pottery, but the Maya potters were women, who sat down at their work. The gods shown are the maize god, a jaguar-deity, the Lord of the North Star, and Itzamna the creator god. Now in the Museo de America, Madrid.

that each part of the world sees only a small proportion of visible eclipses out of the number that actually take place. It is this very exact calculation of events that could *never* be regularly visible in the Maya country which gives one an idea of their astrological genius.

The time-counts in the codices are linked also with figures of gods and show that the Maya calendar was as closely linked with their mythology as that of the more northerly peoples of Mexico. The gods appear in their seasons and hold rule over their various regions of the universe. There are deities of the four directions who stand at the corners of the known world holding up the heavens. They are the four Bacabs who were often represented on stone stelae in ancient times as giant figures holding the bar symbolizing the sun's path in their hands. Among them there stands a goddess who is shown in a dress decorated with jade beads. She represents the southern quarter of the sky, just as a god sometimes shown peeping through a mask of skin and sometimes shown with dried corn stalks on his head represents the direction west. One can recognize the gods on the paintings and on the monuments. Thus we can be quite sure that there was a true continuity of Maya religious and ceremonial life right from the ancient cities of the forest, through to the times of the Yucatec Maya.

From late Maya times, possibly as late as the fifteenth century only a little before the Spanish conquest – we have another book, the *Codex Troano-Cortesianus,* now in Madrid. It also contains calendrical calculations but they are rather less important than in the earlier codices. It has however many interesting details of the agricultural life of the Maya, and tells us of days for planting and sowing, the ritual of the new year ceremonies, and a whole series of fortunate and

Plaster cast prepared by the British archaeologist Alfred P. Maudslay about 1885 from a stucco panel excavated at Palenque, Chiapas. The original panel was made in the seventh century A.D. Among the water lilies can be seen the long-snouted head of the rain god Chac, and the thunder god with his symbolic axe marked on his eye. Such work, painted in natural colours, decorated all the main buildings in the ancient city of Palenque.

unfortunate days for hunting, in which we are shown all manner of hunting devices employed by the Maya. These three documents are all that remains of what was obviously once a very rich painted literature. During their own internal wars the Maya might destroy the books of a captured town, and it was no surprise when the Spaniards came that with the burning of temples went the burning of the books. Later on, the Spanish missionaries were horrified at the presence of the surviving books on heathenism and many of them tried to persuade the local chiefs to destroy them. The Archbishop of Yucatan, Las Casas, commanded that in his district all known ancient painted books should be brought to him. Although he is credited with the wholesale destruction of Maya literature, the fact is that he ordered

the destruction of only nine of these works. The others mostly
perished from neglect, or from constant usage in Maya households.
Three or four historical calendars, which probably had an origin in
Toltec times, since their count of years does not go back beyond the
tenth century, were later written down in the Maya language, but in
Spanish handwriting, and these preserved ancient traditions well into
the eighteenth century. They are known as the books of *Chilan Balam*
after the name of a semi-mythical prophet. The title means the Books
of the Jaguar Priest.

The possession of writing, which was used for books and
monumental inscriptions, does not indicate that all the Maya were
literate. The great majority of people were small farmers and had
no particular reason to read stories of the gods or to learn the detailed
ceremonials of special local festivals by heart. Writing seems to have
been a priestly accomplishment, shared by many of the nobles who
were always, at some point of their career, involved in the priestly
orders. Until the time of the Toltec the Maya appear to have
preserved nothing that can be described as history. It may be that
there was an oral tradition, it may be that there were history books of
which we have no trace; but inscribed monuments known so far
appear to be entirely calendrical and religious in nature without
reference to the great chiefs who commanded them to be produced.

In technology the Maya were very well advanced; we know from
the sculpture, pottery figurines and their books that clothing was most
elaborate, and textiles were woven and dyed in many colours. Their
pottery was good, their stone work speaks for itself, and occasionally

The Maya People

we have some fortunately preserved pieces of woodwork. These are
mostly from interior sections of temples, where they would have been
kept dry, but they are also of Chicozapote wood which is almost
indestructible by the white ant and so had a special chance of survival.
Otherwise we have no material remains of many kinds of carved
wooden objects, the trumpets, the spears, the scepters, and the
thrones with which we are familiar from the sculptures of the older
Maya period. The art of sculpture and of making pottery figurines
continued into Maya-Toltec times but it lost most of its grace and
cultured elegance when it came to reflect the more direct and violent
art which came from Mexico. But even this standard gradually faded
and the pottery figures of the late Maya towns of Yucatan fell terribly
low. It is quite obvious that the potters had skill to make finer figures if
there had been any market for them, but it seems that there was a fashion
for coarse grey pottery of great simplified form. This is vigorous and
strong but, compared to the early work, can only be described as
barbarous. It is like comparing Coptic work of the seventh century
A.D. with the work of 18th Dynasty Egyptians. However, in the case of
the Maya, the change in style occurs in a lapse of time of only a matter
of six centuries. There had been a total subversion of the old art style.

Far left, above:
A pottery figure from an
incense vase. This type of
pottery is characteristic of
the Maya peoples who lived
in the city states which they
built in Yucatan and British
Honduras after the fall of
their older civilisation. The
clay has been mixed with
grit to make sure that it will
not distort during firing.
The figure has been built up
from sheets of clay. Fourteenth or fifteenth century
A.D.

Far left, below:
A late Maya figure which
formed the lid of a large
pottery vessel. The ware is of
finer quality than contemporary work from Yucatan,
and comes from highland
Guatemala. The style of
decoration although sim-
plified shows a continuity
of tradition from more
ancient times. On the surface
can be seen the marks of
careful burnishing which has
resulted in a smooth surface
finish.

Left, above:
A very fine sculptured head
of a jaguar, in a fine-grained
metamorphic rock, of the
Chorotegan people of the
fifteenth century, from the
Nicoya Peninsula, Costa
Rica. This has been ground
and polished into shape with
stone tools. The round portion representing the neck is
drilled through so that the
head can be mounted as a
mace. Presented to the
Cleveland Museum of Art,
in memory of Mr. and Mrs.
Henry Humphreys by their
daughter Helen.

Left, below:
Large pottery vase with
modelled jaguar head and
paws, from the Costa Rica
highlands. Note how the
potter has shaped the arms of
the animal to form two of the
three feet which support the
vase. Fourteenth century
A.D. or a little earlier.
Lankester Collection.

The Maya People

From the beginning of hieroglyphic writing in the early centuries of our era it is clear that the Maya language survived all social changes with only slow and normal variations in dialect. At the time of the Spanish conquest there were six or seven Maya dialects in common use in the area populated by these people and it may well be that we shall find dialectical differences in the older Maya inscriptions. So far as can be seen the nature of the change is steady and slow and we can expect no more difference over six centuries of the Maya tongue than between the English of Chaucer and of modern poets.

Another point of extraordinary continuity was the simple agricultural system, which continued unchanged through the Toltec supremacy, right through the period of Spanish domination, and is even continued today in many Maya villages throughout Yucatan. The reason is that it is simple, practical and produces satisfactory results quite sufficient for feeding the population and leaving a surplus for trade. There was apparently no reason for the Maya to attempt to improve their agriculture.

In the smaller villages one still finds people living in pleasant huts with a wooden framework, and walls usually made of cane–sometimes of wattlework–plastered over with clay and with thatched roofs. These are clean, dry and airy, utterly suitable to the climate, and it is no surprise to find representations on early Maya monuments of many houses of the same kind including more elaborate ones which were apparently used by the chiefs. The temples of the gods had stone houses on top, and it was not until the full development of the early Maya culture that we have great stone buildings, like some of those at Uxmal, which contain rather uncomfortably cramped rooms arranged so that they may have been used as palaces for the nobles. Toltec influence brought the idea of the *tecpan*, or fortified palace in the Mexican tradition, to the Maya country. It had its own development and was only replaced in later times by the Spanish house with its walled courtyards, the *hacienda*–a building of purely European origin which through the practical considerations of life on such a farm, had many points of contact with the Maya-Toltec houses of land-owners.

Among the Maya we have the interesting phenomenon of a people who lost their highest cultural levels, including the arts of painting and sculpture, but who preserved a way of life and a language which gave them a strong sense of unity and which has stayed with them until modern times. Of the Maya of the forest we have little history. After the Spanish invasion there was some resistance among the independent Itzá in the southern region, but this faded out, and the forests were left to be occupied only by wandering bands of hunting people who, although true Maya, were extremely poor in their culture. These Lacandones, who have recently been filmed, have been subjected to attempts to bring them into regular settlements. It seems as if this will be the signal for their disappearance as a separate people, and they will probably become part of the general Maya-speaking inhabitants of Guatemala and southern Mexico.

Of recorded Maya history we have nothing. Yet in their cultural history they are unique in that they maintained a racial tradition which continued for 2,000 years, and of which we have very full evidence concerning building, agriculture, social custom and so on. It is only paralleled among other nations by the continuous cultural tradition of the Chinese.

Above:
A young man of the Kash-inaua tribe of Amazonia. His feather ornaments represent full dress for ceremonial occasions. In ancient times the traders from Inca Peru exchanged cloth and carvings for such feather ornaments, as well as for jaguar skins and monkeys.

Left:
Father and son in a fibre hammock with their pet spider monkey. Waura Indians of Amazonia. In common with many of the forest Indians these people practice the couvade. The custom tends to strengthen family ties, and to bring the father into closer sympathy with his children.

Right:
Kraho Indian men painted for the dance. Note the elder man has removed his ear-plugs for the painting and his ear lobe hangs in a loop. The younger, more fashion-able man, wears a little square of cloth over his penis. Both wear dancing belts in which nut shells hang on strings to give a musical rattle with every movement.

The Peoples Between

The isthmus of Central America was never such a highway from Mexico to Peru as it appears on a map. By tracing the linguistic divisions among the various Indian groups who were living there in the sixteenth century we can see that they had already been disrupted and changed around in a way which indicates that there had been a long history of tribal wars and invasions in earlier centuries. In particular the Chibcha-speaking tribes were broken into several sections in what is now Panama and Costa Rica quite apart from the main body of their nation in the highlands of Colombia. In Nicaragua and even as far south as Costa Rica traces of Nahuatl languages show that some tribes were of a Mexican origin in the past.

This violent mixing and division of populations may well be attributed to the rugged mountains and heavy forests of the isthmus. It was almost impossible for any towns and villages of any given tribe to keep in continuous contact. Invasions were forced to follow devious routes. Communications were easily broken off, and so the archaeological diversity of the region reflects the confusion which must have marked tribal history.

Opposed to the broken land communications was a sea route which linked Florida with the forests of Amazonia by way of the West Indian islands. There is a little evidence that some communication existed between Florida and the northern islands. Some artifacts of West Indian origin have been found in the north, and there are some ancient and primitive island cultures which present a North American aspect. But for the last two milennia the general advance of canoe-borne peoples seems to have been from South America towards the Carribean and thence in successive waves of invasion into the islands. This sea route was too far away from the high civilizations of Peru for them to have made any contact with either Mexican or Mayan civilizations. In fact tnere is at present no direct evidence to show that even the enterprising Maya coastal towns had any contact with the simple villagers of the islands.

The story of the West Indians really commenced at some unknown period in South America, where canoe-using tribes speaking the Tupí language spread from the region of Paraguay through the river systems, and then northwards along the coast of Brazil. They never formed a united national group, but formed large villages where they cultivated manioc, cassava and the sweet potato. At first they had few

Above:
A golden water-pot from the Chimú Kingdom of the northern coast of Peru; probably thirteenth or fourteenth century A.D. It is possible that the arch between the two spouts represents the heavens, perhaps the rainbow which was worshipped in Peru in ancient times. In the centre is the head of a deity wearing a helmet, flanked by two lesser deities. On the body of the vessel, deer are standing beneath the sky as if on a mountain; at the sides are two heads of an animal usually identified with a stylised puma, but in this case the horns on the heads cannot be explained. Whether they are cult symbols, or derived from some other civilisation is not clear. The vessel was found in the heartland of Chimú culture, the Lambayeque district.
Right:
A gold cone-shaped vase of the same culture. The decorations are of turquoise. Mujica Gallo Collection, Lima.

A large stone head, of Tiahuanaco design, now in La Paz, Bolivia. This is a typical piece of the cubic art of the later period of the Tiahuanaco culture. The surface decoration, closely akin to textile motifs, points the meaning of the sculpture.

110

stone tools, but as they moved into regions where stone was abundant more and more stone axes and adzes were made.

The Indians of the Amazon forests apparently never reached the Stone Age. Their abundant supplies of wood and cane were all that were necessary for a comfortable life. They have, naturally enough, no archaeology, although a few potsherds may eventually serve as a clue to tribal movements in ancient times. The greatest cultural advance of any of the tribes was made by the peoples of Marajo Island at the mouth of the Amazon. They were expert potters and have left many beautifully decorated vessels which hint at distant influences coming from the Andean cultures. From this island and the immediate neighbourhood have come green stone pendants representing fertility frogs, small and beautiful, and exceedingly rare and precious today.

Around the coasts the Tupí-speaking tribes steadily pushed forward. It probably took centuries for the more adventurous waves of them to reach Venezuela. Before them other tribes fled north to the farther islands. Thus it comes about that at the beginning of the Christian era the West Indies were already being populated. In Cuba a primitive and early population called the Ciboney have been traced by their pottery and stone tools, and these may represent an original invasion of the islands from the north. But the real advance came from the South American mainland, and the people who moved in first with a settled agricultural village life were the Taino. The name comes from a word they first used when meeting Christopher Columbus: *Taino!* (peace).

Their tools were polished from diorite and other hard rock. They lived by the cultivation of maize, manioc, and, interestingly, sugar cane. The home of the sugar cane is on these larger West Indian islands.

A young married lady of the Maku Indians of the Japura River in Amazonas State, Brazil. In this humid forest climate clothing is of little value, but she would feel deeply shocked if the leg rings worn just below her knee were removed. They are symbols of her grown-up status, and serve to thicken her calves as a sign of beauty. Her husband has made her a most important gift of the necklace with great jaguar fangs from animals he has killed himself.

Young men of the Kraho Indians of Goiaz State, Brazil. They have been on an expedition to catch fish, for which they have used a poison made by mashing a creeper with a juice which is toxic to fish and harmless to man.

The Peoples Between

Stone pestle of sixteenth century type, Taino Culture, from the Greater Antilles, perhaps Cuba. The male figure appears to represent a boy. It is not known whether these pestles were used ordinarily for crushing roots such as cassava for food or whether they had a ceremonial purpose.

Carved stone representing a female squatting figure. Fifteenth century, Taino Culture, probably from Santo Domingo. Such stones represent the Zemis (spirit powers) worshipped by the Indians in the time of Columbus.

The Taino people made fine wood carvings and knew how to work gold, which they called *guanin*. The Spanish discoverers of the island soon tried to enslave the natives and reduced them nearly to extinction, and of all the treasures of gold which are described in the chronicles nothing remains, with the exception of the inlaid eyes and mouth of a head carved on a small wooden stool now preserved in the British Museum; otherwise the ancient treasures of the West Indies have disappeared.

The Taino were followed up from South America by canoes containing parties of Caribs. These were the original *Carribales*, as the Spaniards called them; cannibals, in fact. From this race came the famous Man Friday of *Robinson Crusoe*. The Caribs literally ate their way into the islands, and occupied all the smaller islands in the southern part of the Caribbean Sea in the two centuries before the arrival of the Spaniards. Most of the Taino men were killed and eaten, and the women taken as wives, and this resulted in the curious case of men and boys speaking the full Carib language but women speaking among themselves a completely different dialect which was related to the old Taino languages of their ancestors. The Caribs were magnificent canoe carvers, at least according to Columbus and other early Spanish voyagers, and also very good workers in stone. We know this from the elaborate stone pendants, axe blades, and ceremonial objects of unknown use, found in the parts of the islands which the Caribs occupied.

Apart from these races there was no other kind of civilization in the West Indies. Both in language and in culture the islanders differed widely from the Indians of the mainland. In some ways they are more closely related to the Tupí Indians of the coasts of Brazil than to any other American peoples.

There is some slight evidence of West Indian contact with the coastal regions of Florida. The Lucayans of the Bahamas made very beautiful tools entirely from shell, as there was no workable stone on their islands. Their fishermen appear to have visited the Florida coast and to have taken there stone axes and even small carvings which they obtained no doubt by trading with the Taino tribes farther south. However, this was the only kind of contact between the West Indies and North America.

The true region of the isthmus, which contains Panama, is even more confused archaeologically than Costa Rica. There were apparently many agricultural tribes of varying levels of culture. Some of them worked pearl fisheries. Archaeological evidence does not go back beyond the Christian era as yet, but it is certain that the region was inhabited very much earlier since it was a cultural crossroads between North and South America. One suspects that in ancient times the traders who exchanged ideas as well as goods went farthest by canoe. Also convoys of traders were travelling inland with packs on their backs from one place to another, for there were no beasts of burden available in this country. The tribes did not bother to make roads because, after all, the man with a pack on his back is much more comfortable on earthen paths than on stone paved roads. There was little contact between each area apart from this small-scale trade.

Art styles differ considerably, and they are all surprisingly advanced. Finely decorated pottery was made in several areas. Elaborate figures of gods and sacred animals decorated the pots, and appear again in a mass of beautiful gold work which every village seemed to be able to produce at will. Some of these tribes knew how to get gold from the rocks by roasting powdery red cinnabar to produce mercury and then washing the gold bearing rock until the mercury and gold had formed into a spongy yellow amalgam. They placed the new substance in a pottery vessel which was heated on a fire, driving the mercury off as a poisonous vapour and leaving behind a spongy mass of gold. It was then either melted down, or hammered and burnished into the desired shape. This was a technical advance, unique in the ancient Americas. Attractive stone pendants were also made which acted as anchorages for further elaborations of this beautiful work.

But in spite of all their skills tribal states appear never to have grown into nations. Sometimes a cluster of a dozen or so villages scattered over twenty or thirty miles have such great similarities in culture that we must reckon that there was a unified government, but it never seems to have controlled a large area.

As one proceeds southwards from Panama, there is a development of civilization, particularly as one ascends towards the main ranges of the Andes. On the Pacific Coast there are still to be found cultures, even as far south as the Manabí peninsula in Ecuador, which show some relationship with Mexican art, while on the Atlantic coast the level of civilization rapidly decreases as one approaches the confines of the great forest lands.

In Venezuela there were more primitive tribes of Indians who made only small pottery figurines, and lived in comfortable hutments often built on stilts over the waters of the Gulf of Maracaibo. It was this custom which induced the first Spanish voyagers to that country to call it *Venezuela*, which simply means Little Venice.

Towards the northern coast of Colombia there were other more highly organized tribes who depended on fishing and maize agriculture for their food, but who also grew a great deal of cotton and cultivated cacao for the cocoa beans. These people were the Tairona. They organized towns in which the houses were sometimes connected with paved paths. Every Tairona town was a network of streets around the rectangular stone bases on which their comfortable tropical huts were erected. They made a coarse type of pottery often with elaborate surface decoration, and sometimes modelled animal figures. The local clay from which their pots were made had a remarkably low temperature for firing, and the potters must have had a considerable knowledge to produce vessels which did not crumble because they were overheated. The Tairona themselves were great sea traders; their canoes travelled north towards the isthmus of Panama on the one side, and east along the coast of Venezuela on the other.

As we have seen, the really expert canoemen of the South American coasts did not travel to the isthmus, probably because of the superior power of people like the Tairona near the Gulf of Maracaibo. Their path was easiest towards the fertile islands of the West Indies. To the south of Maracaibo, the Andes spread eastwards into a high plateau with less massive vegetation than in the hinterland of Venezuela. The region contains some volcanic lakes, and by reason of the river valleys has trails leading through hilly country into the forests.

The climate of the Andean plateau was more helpful to man than that of the great forest. In the eastern plateau one group in particular,

Stone pestle carved with a human head showing a pattern of face paint, and circular earrings of a type seen in wooden images from Jamaica. There may once have been an inlay of shell, or even gold in the eyes. West Indian Taino Culture, fourteenth or fifteenth century A.D.

115

the Muisca, one of the Chibcha-speaking peoples whose languages were spoken in parts of Panama and right into the highlands of Colombia, developed a civilization around the present town of Bogotá. Their chiefs had records which seem to have gone back several generations. The Muisca were under the administration of an autocratic high chief who was chosen from the most capable of the younger men of the ruling family. On his accession he was powdered with gold dust and made to jump into the sacred lake of Guatavita, where the gold dust was washed off of his skin and sank slowly in the water as an offering to the golden serpents, thought to be the first ancestors of mankind and believed to be still living at the bottom of the lake. This great chief, the *El Dorado* (The Gilded One) as the Spaniards called him, administered a country where many gods were worshipped, but principally Bochica the Sun God. The towns were large villages of wooden houses with stone foundations, sometimes connected with paved pathways. The palace of the great chief was larger than other houses and decorated with a good deal of gold and tumbaga.

The warriors of the Muisca occasionally raided far afield, certainly as far as the Guyanas. Their search was not for treasure or for food but for beautiful boys who could be captured and kept for sacrifice to Bochica the Sun God. If any of the boys could get away and escape into the same hut in which a girl was living he was allowed to marry and escape being sacrificed to the sun. However the watch was so careful that this rarely happened. Everywhere these Chibcha-speaking warriors went they carried with them golden images of Bochica in the form of an eagle, which they hung around their neck by a string of cotton. It was one of these eagles that Sir Walter Raleigh obtained by trade from the Indians in Guyana. Later, when imprisoned in the Tower of London, he regularly wore this around his neck as mute evidence that his search for gold and treasure in South America had reality behind it. However it did not save his life.

Farther to the west there were deep river valleys in which several Colombian tribes erected small towns, each of which appears to have had its independent chief. They met each other in occasional bloodthirsty forays, from which prisoners were taken home in triumph to be killed and eaten by the victors. The towns were protected by stockade fences and were usually no more than a cluster of small cane-walled and thatched houses, but the inhabitants possessed a remarkable skill in metal work. They had copper ore in abundance, a great deal of placer gold which they washed out of river sands, and a good deal of platinum. In fact in some parts of the country platinum was so common that it was hammered out and made into fish hooks for use in the rapid flowing rivers of the mountains.

Gold was not only made into alloys with the other metals but sometimes used in its pure state, made into very beautiful pendants worn around the necks of warriors. The more important among these tribes were the Sinú who preferred geometric structure in their art; and the Quimbaya, who made exquisite ornaments of gold and copper mixture with surface enrichment. They knew how to melt gold and copper together to make a strong alloy which they moulded into near realistic representations of human figures, frogs and other small animal forms. Some of these ornaments were used as rings, some were spear throwers, some were ceremonial ornaments for the temples beside the houses of their chiefs. Figures and vases up to ten or twelve inches in

A small tumbaga (gold and copper alloy – the surface copper is removed to leave only the gold) figure of the Tairona culture of Colombia. About six inches high, its true purpose is not known. It might have been purely ornamental, though the strange head suggests a votive offering in an animal cult. The culture lasted for about 500 years from the tenth century A.D.

height were quite frequently made. The brilliant and smooth golden finish was obtained by washing the surface of the alloy with a vegetable acid which was sharp enough to dissolve a great deal of the outer face of the copper from the alloy and leave a surface of almost pure gold. This, after a thorough washing, was burnished with smooth pebbles until it shone; giving the appearance of a totally golden object, smooth and brilliant in texture.

The figures of the more important people are always shown as quite naked apart from tattoo patterns. It was considered that common people working in the fields, growing maize and picking fruits, needed some kind of clothing to protect themselves from brambles and insects; but the higher class, who spent more time in their houses and received tributes from the commoners, wore no clothing whatever. They bothered considerably about the richness of their tattoos and the beautiful smoothness of their skin; so they were represented in the images simply as natural and really rather lovely human beings. In a few cases masks are found which reflect a curious evil quality which goes well with the outrageous cannibalism of these tribes, who even occasionally bred children for the purpose of eating the softer flesh when they were a year or so old. Such practices were not totally unknown in other cannibal societies; but among these cultured, gold-working people of the Quimbaya culture, this kind of cultivated cannibalism was a regular custom. One can imagine the savagery with which the Spanish soldiers assaulted the villages after witnessing such atrocious deeds.

The highland cities and political states of the Quimbaya and Muisca cannot be compared in importance with either the Cara or Inca dominions. However, they had such wealth and culture of their own that they are of considerable interest in their own right. Their basic economy depended upon cultivation of the maize plant which had come down from Mexico through the isthmus. Maize had already reached Peru by 1,000 B.C. and so it must have been cultivated in these northern highland regions even earlier. The climate of this whole region was moist. The westerly winds meant that rain came from the Pacific, and the coast land was not a great desert as in Peru. The whole of the mountains were covered by forest both on the plateau and both sides of the Cordilleras. This made communication difficult, so intensifying the separation which prevented the formation of any unified state of importance north of Peru, except upon the plateau around Bogotá where the Muisca people built up their own simple civilization.

We have no clue about the speed with which maize cultivation spread from one tribe to another in the distant past, but we can understand why trade was very restricted in the regions north of Peru. The routes presented great difficulties in transport, only a few narrow trackways passed south from the many different regions of Colombia into Ecuador. South of Manabí the Ecuadorian coast was inhabited only by wild forest Indians, because this tropical coast above the equator has such heavy rainfall that it is a region of dense forest and swampy coastal jungle. The inhabitants at all times have been primitive tribes mostly living by fishing and a certain amount of agriculture in their small village gardens. But still farther south was the powerful kingdom of the Cara whose chief the Scyri of Quito became a tributary to the Inca Empire in Peru.

Ceremonial knife of cast and soldered plates of gold-copper alloy. The blade is of bronze overlaid with gold in a process akin to Sheffield plating. The central figure is a deity, though whether of sun or moon is uncertain. He is supported by curious bird-man figures. All the figures of human form wear the typical South American Indian leg-bands. Sixteenth century A.D. or earlier, from the region of Popayan, Colombia.

GULF OF
MARACAIBO

TRINIDAD

Lake Maracaibo

Orinoco River

VENEZUELA   GUYANA   FRENCH
                                   GUIANA

Bogotá   SURINAM

TOLIMA

COLOMBIA   MARAJO ISLAND

Quito   Amazon River

ECUADOR

MANABI PENINSULA

PERU

Marañon River

Cupisnique Valley

Cajamarca   B R A Z I L

Chan Chan

Chavin de Huantar

Paramonga   MATTO GROSSO

Lima
Pachacamac   Machu Picchu
Huari
Sacsahuaman   Cuzco
Paraccas   Kenko

Nasca
                   Lake Titicaca

Tiahuanaco   La Paz

                   BOLIVIA

                                   PARAGUAY
C
H
I
L   T
E   H
       E
       A
       N   GRAN CHACO
       D
       E   URUGUAY
       S

                                   ARGENTINA

PACIFIC OCEAN   ATLANTIC OCEAN

                   Rio de la Plata

                   PATAGONIA

118

MAGELLAN'S STRAIT

The Beginnings of Civilisation in Peru

Pottery portrait vase representing a seated warrior. The red-ware body has been painted over with a pale cream-coloured slip; the dark areas are covered with a clay slip containing iron oxide which has produced a reddish-brown colour. The pot was fired after the slip had been applied. The warrior wears an axe-blade in front of his helmet, and has a club lying underneath his shield. The art of portraiture among the Mochica people was an original discovery, owing nothing to other cultures. This figure is a fine example and dates from about the fourth century A.D.

Throughout the long ages when mankind in America was progressing slowly towards the building of small towns and villages, settlements in Peru were unusually fortunate. In the highlands there were wild plants suitable for food including quinoa (a good seed-bearing plant), beans and wild potatoes. On the coast things were different. The land surface was fertile in very early times, but slow erosion made it into a howling desert broken only by small valleys cut by streams rushing down from the mountains. The flood plains of these small valleys were fertile and crops of beans and squash were cultivated with some success. There also appears to have been a cotton plant but whether this was introduced or whether it was a wild native of Peru is still uncertain.

The villages along the coast of Peru had an inexhaustible supply of food from the sea. The cool Humboldt current, sweeping along the coast of South America from Antarctica, brings with it myriads of fish. These in turn are the food of a wide variety of animals and birds including the large sea birds which were also eaten. This land was so rich that there must have been considerable leisure for the development of civilization in coastal areas. Another factor was the division caused by the desert. Trouble between different villages could not so easily result in armed conflict when travel between the homes of different chiefs was so hard. Clashes of culture were only possible when civilization had developed to a fairly high degree. Similarly in the highlands, the rugged mountain barriers between the valleys in which people lived divided the tribes. They too had to advance a long way from the stage of primitive agriculture to the point where they became interested in territorial acquisitions, and were able to make good their claims by imposing their rule over other small towns and villages.

The crucial point in the development of these early cultures appears to have occurred about 2,000 B.C. Previously a pre-ceramic culture appears to have existed and with it some forms of art. Weaving began with twining and developed quite elaborate patterns. Rough clay unbaked models slowly gave place to fired clay objects and the development of portable vessels. The small villages of 2,000 B.C. rapidly became larger and ceremonial centres were set aside both for the worship of the gods and for the burial of dead citizens. The process then accelerates and about 900 B.C. we find the development of cultures which have well-organized commerce, fine pottery and complexes of buildings which indicate the existence of a highly organized religion. This seems to have begun in the highland valleys, in regions where there was contact with the rich jungles of the Amazon forest and also with the fruitful plateau where grain could be cultivated, and where the wild llama and alpaca were to be found in vast numbers.

The apparent focus of this culture was the temple of Chavín. It was roughly a solid mass of masonry containing narrow passageways. The walls were decorated by large stone sculptured heads of people and animals which were set firmly in the stone wall surface by means of tenons. Within the passageways many elaborate carvings are to be found, including one that is actually pendant from the ceiling like an artificial stalactite. The people of the Chavín culture were fascinated by ferocious earth dieties. Jaguar masks, and figures with basically human form but jaguar features, sometimes with several superimposed heads, appear to represent some terrifying god who devours men and tears off their heads. There are also large dragon-like creatures who may represent an early form of the Earth-Mother spirit, thus making a primitive duality of the surface and the interior of the fruitful earth. From our point of view these carvings represent dangerous creatures of alarming ferocity, but of course there is no reason to think that they were really anything of the sort to the people who carved their images. The aesthetics of sculpture may differ radically in widely different social surroundings.

Pottery from Ecuador and Colombia. These cultures show affinities, as yet unexplained, with ancient Mexican art. Left: a pottery figure from the Esmeraldas region of the Ecuadorean coast. Centre: a carved pottery vessel from the Quimbaya tribes of the Cauca River Valley of central Colombia. Right: a vessel with supporting figures, from the Chibcha-speaking Muisca of the plateau region around Bogotá. The Esmeraldas figure dates from before 1000 A.D. The Colombian vessels are fourteenth century A.D.

The Beginning of Civilization in Peru

The coastal civilizations of Peru at this early period developed mostly in the southern half of what is now the area of the Peruvian Republic. The most important site was at Paraccas. Here there is little trace of any town settlement, but two cemeteries have been found in which the methods of burial were strikingly different. In one the bodies are buried in comparatively simple bundles and accompanied by most beautifully decorated pottery, and in the other the bodies are enwrapped in embroidered mantles of fantastic complexity of design but are accompanied only by well-modelled but extremely plain and simple ceramics. These two cultures have something in common but it appears that the one with the decorated pottery and plain textiles is somewhat earlier. The pottery is distinguished by incised designs on a grey body. Colour areas on the surface are divided by the incised lines and the colour produced by rubbing in bright colours: red, yellow, blue and green. The subjects of design are rather similar to the stone carvings found far away to the north east in Chavín. How these possibly mythological ideas and art styles were spread is not quite clear. It may be that the American Indian temperament at this period was formulating similar religious concepts in widely separate areas. It is a fact that there is a basic artistic tradition in American Indian things which would allow for the general similarity of design.

However, within the fully developed Paraccas Cavernas culture a similar mythology is expressed with stronger local influences and infinitely greater richness in the form of multicoloured embroideries on a simple woven base cloth. Some of these enormous cloths which formed the outer coverings for dried bodies, presumably of local chiefs, may be as large as twenty by fifteen feet. These pieces of cloth were woven with a very simple under-and-over weave but totally covered by brilliantly coloured embroideries. These embroideries are sometimes of cotton, sometimes of llama wool. The cotton, of course, was more suitable for dyeing and we have examples in which red, yellow, two shades of green, purple and a greyish blue are all used. The amount of time taken in covering one of the huge mantles with a multitude of small embroidered figures, and even embroidered background patterns, is so enormous that one must think of a woman spending several years in preparing each of these wonderful robes, which appear to have been used only in funeral services. This, however, is by no means certain, and one must think that the great chiefs wore elaborate robes embroidered in similar fashion during their normal lifetime.

A large pottery vessel from excavations in the island of Marajo at the mouth of the Amazon. The complex designs carved on the bowl after firing are similar to those used by Amazonian Indians for decoration of wooden objects and for painting their bodies. Red pottery painted over before firing with a deeper reddish slip, probably fifteenth or sixteenth century.

Two golden pendants of almost pure metal, with a deliberately designed matt surface. These little creatures represent the first human ancestors, who at the destruction of a previous world had been turned into water serpents to survive the flood which the sun god Bochica intended should destroy the earth. They disappeared with the last water from the flood into the crater lake of Guatavita, and their human descendants inherited the new earth. Muisca work from near Bogota, Colombia. Fifteenth century A.D.

The Beginning of Civilization in Peru

The gods of the Paraccas people, as they appear on the textiles, are almost entirely spirits of nature. We find serpents of many kinds, some with human heads; enormous catlike creatures, some shown as yellow, some striped; and occasionally birds. These all appear to reflect the world of nature as seen by the Paraccas artists. In every case nature was felt to be instinct with a life of its own and occasionally its terrible aspects are emphasized. Not one of the animals shown is a creature that we should think of as timid or helpless, they have all become symbols of types of the powerful animals which at times can be dangerous. We must conclude that this growing religion in Peru was based in the dependence of man on the forces of the world around him. The farmers, the hunters, and the builders were all subject from time to time to natural catastrophe. These in their sudden appearance can be likened to the powers of great earth-monsters, of jaguars on the mountains and of the condors swooping from the sky. However, this fear of nature did not prevent its utilization by man. The Indians of the Paraccas culture were quite obviously farmers of great skill who cultivated their own foodstuffs, including maize, which had infiltrated into Peru from the north, and grew cotton for textiles.

On the southern coast of Peru about 200 B.C. the Paraccas culture was succeeded quite gently by a civilization from which, again, we have so far but few remains of towns or buildings. However, this Nasca culture was highly efficient from the technological point of view. The people continued the Paraccas traditions in design, especially on textiles, but their technical ability had advanced tremendously. Instead of overall embroidery we find that they had developed a true tapestry technique in which the patterns are created by the use of different coloured threads woven in the fabric on the loom. The looms

The Beginning of Civilization in Peru

Far left:
Panel from a painted textile showing Bochica, the sun god of the Chibcha-speaking Muisca people of Colombia. The simplicity of design shows the characteristic aesthetic of Chibcha art. This is the only piece of Chibcha cloth known to exist, and until recently was believed to be of Inca origin. Fifteenth century A.D. British Museum.

were still very simple constructions which were tied to a tree at one end and at the other fixed by a belt around the waist of the weaver. Between the weaver and the support were two loom bars on which the warp threads were spread. The weft was thrown on by a spindle for which the passage was cleared by simple hand-worked heddles. This is the most primitive loom known to man, and it was never elaborated in the whole history of Peru, so that even in the time of the Incas women were using the same primitive type of weaving to produce the most gorgeous textiles imaginable.

The Nasca people also applied decoration to pottery. From pottery models of humans we see that the decoration extended into face paint and indeed little patterns all over the body. There is one charming little pottery figurine of a naked girl who has patterns on her cheeks, on her elbows, around her wrists, on her knees, across the lower part of her pelvic region, and on her ankles. Apparently she was equipped with the equivalent of a set of heavy jewellery by the simple process of painting it, or stamping it, on her skin. Grown-up ladies wore long gowns of natural creamy white cotton and capes over their shoulders. Men wore thick loincloths, wrapped around them to make something like little swimming trunks. Occasionally one finds a figure which is almost certainly male, wearing a round cap and a long straight robe, so we may take it that normal dress among the Nasca was the long gown. This was an excellent costume in the hot, dry daytime climate of this desert coast. It allowed air to circulate freely about the body, and screened the skin from the violence of hot sunshine which in these tropical latitudes, by the salty sea-coast, could really be harmful.

The work produced by the Nasca people always shows a high degree of skill. They seemed to have taken great trouble not only with

Left:
The deserts of the Peruvian coast. This apparently life-less land was nonetheless the scene of remarkable cultural activity—a few small rivers run down from the mount-ains and these were exploited to a remarkable degree by the Indians of the region, who were experts in the art of irrigation.

Carved stone head of human and feline nature, probably an earth deity. The head is set in the outer wall of the early temple at Chavín de Huantar. About 900 B.C.

123

A Paraccas figurine, with incised decoration and conical headdress. Kemper Collection.

weaving and with personal decoration but in every instrument that they made. Their spear throwers are nicely formed and often engraved. Their stone axe-blades were well-shaped and carefully ground. But above all the Nasca excelled in ceramics. Their pottery is usually hand-coiled, although some of it seems to have been made in moulds. And like all other American Indian peoples they were without knowledge of the potter's wheel. The finished Nasca bowls and vases are very fine red ware, coiled precisely and smoothed down to a thickness of about an eighth of an inch, sometimes even less. They were probably fired at temperatures of a little less than 95° C, and this has produced a hard ware which rings pleasantly when tapped.

The remarkable thing about the Nasca pottery, however, is the wide range of colour which was used in decorating it. The potters prepared slips from clay mixed with various natural rocks which included many kinds of metallic oxides. This slip was then painted on the pottery, and a second firing changed the pale tinted creamy slip into the rich colours which we see today. It is probable that the main designs on the pots were first painted in colour, and the black outlines in manganese were painted on afterwards so as to trim the rough edges of the colour. The effect is always precise and always beautiful. To the modern eye the selection of colour is charming. There are backgrounds occasionally of sharp white but mostly of cream colour and a whole series of tones rather than colours, which vary from a soft red through a greyish purple on to greens–dark quiet greens to brown of various shades and onto a soft rosy red and bright yellow. With this quite exceptional range of colour the Nasca artists could produce works of great elegance. They preferred designs from the world of nature. We find pepper pods commonly painted, lima beans are shown held up by little spirits in the form of human beings– apparently the little gods who made the beans grow to nourish mankind. Animals appear–wild cats, llamas, and small deer. A number of centipedes and serpents of various kinds are shown, for the beautiful colour on the serpents and indeed on lizards attracted the Nasca people with their sense of beauty of colour and design. The bird life of Peru also gave them an immense number of themes. We find little finches going about stealing the grain, and humming birds among the flowers. The hawks are painted with patterns around their eyes marking the different species. An occasional condor appears although he, like the llama, seems to have been a design-form imported from the highland people in the mountains away from the coast. This beautiful artwork was used for everyday vessels as far as we know; it is true that all these coloured pots were found in cemeteries, but the main point is that no other pots have been found which give any indication of a separate secular art.

Undoubtedly Nasca people were good farmers and this was due to their ability to utilize the water from the little rivers which here and there rushed through the coastal deserts from the edges of the Andean mountain chain. These streams spread out into small natural delta regions and the Nasca people conducted the water through irrigation channels to increase the size of the delta and so produce more in the way of maize, beans, squash and, of course, cotton, which they used in great quantity for their textiles.

Nasca textiles continue Paraccas design traditions but they develop the forms of gods and demons with much greater freedom,

124

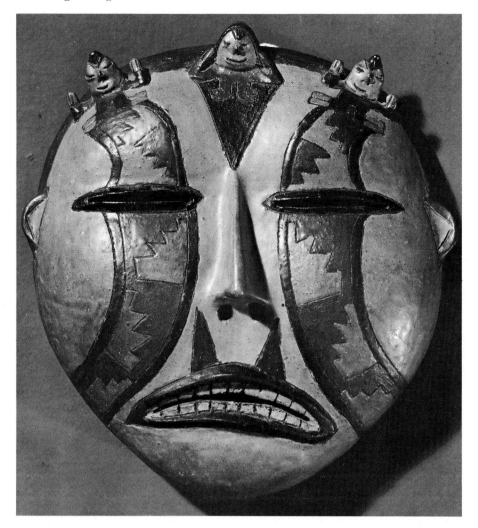

A mask of the Paraccas people of the south coastal region of Peru. Pottery, poly-chromed with post-fired resin paint, it dates from the first century B.C.

partly because of their adoption of true tapestry techniques. The pieces of cloth are never so big as the Paraccas ones, and the general appearance of the work is very much more friendly and gay. In fact one has the feeling that the whole of Nasca art was developed for the expression of the world of nature around. The demon-like creatures are less frightening and, in their animal forms, assume a grace which is much more consistent with the appearance of the real creatures. The great powers which terrify men seem to be personified by human-like forms who wear loin cloth and tunic, carry clubs and stone-bladed axes, and sometimes disport trophies made out of human heads which they carry in their hands or attached to their garments. Some of the gods, however, simply hold plants and seem to be the spirits of the growth in nature which produces food for mankind. The elements of strength, terror and violence are not everywhere apparent, so that one feels that this is a distinct step in civilization reflected in the religious art of the people.

War was apparently fairly common. A few real trophy heads; dried human heads hacked off enemies, have been found; many more are modelled in pottery. The strange weapon used by the Nasca people, a long club with a stone axe blade set in the middle of it, has survived until recent times more than a thousand miles away on the

125

other side of the Andes among the Jivaro Indians of southern Ecuador. And it is interesting that it is these particular people who wear shrunken heads as ornaments on their clothing for great ceremonies, in the same way that the Nasca people used to go on the far-away coasts of southern Peru. However, the Nasca people had not learnt the art of cutting the skull out of the flesh and then shrinking the head until it becomes only the size of a clenched fist. The Nasca heads are simply dried and pierced at the top so that a loop can be fixed for hanging. They must have served the purpose of terrifying enemy groups. Who these enemies were we have no clue, it may be that people from one valley occasionally fought people from the next valley over food, or irrigation rights. Hundreds of little quarrels which can spring up in any small farming community become wars through rivalry with another community in times of shortage.

In later times the Nasca were to be subverted by some kind of invasion from the great centre of Tiahuanaco in the highlands.

The Altiplano, the extraordinary tableland which extends from the north of Peru to the south of Bolivia at an elevation of 12,000 feet. Bleak and treeless at this height it is also subject to the blazing tropical sun. This was the home of the races who founded the great civilizations of Tiahuanaco and the Incas.

This great city with many buildings having frameworks of stone was the centre of a civilization from the beginning of the Christian era until the seventh or eighth centuries A.D. Apparently it developed its own style of art, although this is within the basic tradition which started at Chavín and Paraccas.

Tiahuanaco was not of great importance outside its own highland region until the last two centuries of its power. When the Tiahuanaco irruption occurred along the coast it marked a change from the ancient traditions of the Nasca people. They still used the same technology but gradually altered the designs used in their art, until the Tiahuanaco epigonal style became totally dominant. But when Tiahuanaco collapsed quite suddenly in the eighth century there was no continuity of civilization in the south. Small towns with individual styles of art arose, all rather feeble when compared to the glories of the work of Nasca and even epigonal times. Actually one can be certain

The Beginning of Civilization in Peru

that the early southern cultures in Peru came to a sudden and violent end, so violent that the survivors of the catastrophe ceased to work in the old style and produced something utterly distinct thereafter.

Altogether earlier cultures on the northern coast of Peru were already in existence and producing very fine artwork, it is perhaps best to deal with the Tiahuanaco culture here before we move northwards to consider the civilization known as Mochica. Of the beginnings of Tiahuanaco itself we have no record. This great city, of which the remains of enormous religious constructions survive near Lake Titicaca, was a centre of culture for a few centuries before its warriors captured the coastland. Its artistic traditions bear some relationship with those of Chavín far to the north of Paraccas on the coast of Peru, but they developed in a new way. The Tiahuanaco people were apparently fascinated by the possibility of fitting patterns into squares. They even squared out stone monoliths and fitted forms of gods and warriors on them in square pattern blocks treating each face of a solid monolith as a separate area of sculpture, although all combined to make up the semblance of a figure of four outward surfaces each joined together.

A woman working on her back-strap loom. She is using shed sticks and a single handworked heddle. On such simple looms all the wonderfully complex fabrics of ancient Peru were woven by hand. From the manuscript of Huaman Poma de Ayala.

Nevertheless this work has great strength and dignity, quite consistent with the power which made Tiahuanaco the first imperial state in South America. Who the chiefs were or what was the name of the people who ruled at Tiahuanaco we are by no means sure. It is possible that these were the Colla people, ruled over by a line of chiefs whose title was Amauta or wise man. But this comes only from a single Inca tradition relayed after the Spanish conquest by Father Montesinos. He tells that the Incas had come to Cuzco from the far south where they had descended from a line of well over a hundred chiefs who were known as the Amautas. However, there is no certainty about this tradition. Artistically there is one religious link between Tiahuanaco and Cuzco, the capital of the Incas. At the Gateway of the Sun at Tiahuanaco which was definitely part of the original holy city at that site, the figure of the Sun-god is shown clad in tunic and belt of a basic style similar to that worn by the Incas themselves, and the face of this god is marked by tears running from the eye over the cheek. This design also appears in Tiahuanaco textiles and it illustrates the Inca legend that gold was the tears of the sun. It was because of this that the Incas, who claimed descent from Inti the sun god, had control of all gold within their empire. However that may be, Tiahuanaco is marked by its own style; the Gateway of the Sun is undoubtedly symbolic of the heavens. The sun god in the centre is surrounded by rays ending in the heads of condors and great puma-headed serpents. In his hands he carries the equivalent of Jove's thunderbolts; these are lightning serpents, and arrows with condor heads, in other words the sun god is living in a blaze of light from which he sends the powers of lightning. On either side of them there are dozens of little winged figures, each one carrying a lightning staff and shown in a curious position which can be interpreted either as running or kneeling. It seems that these must be the stars of the sky. Both above and below in woven bands of pattern one finds other strange creatures which may well represent the planets in their paths among the stars.

We are confronted with a civilization which had great interest in astronomy. This need not, however, surprise us because on the coast the Nasca people had already made great alignments of white stones on plateaus on the hills above the coast which bear directly towards the rising and setting points of certain stars. They include among them representations of birds which are almost certainly the planets. The reason for all this interest in astronomy is quite simple. The farmer may know very well when to reap his crops, but on which particular day is he to plant them to get the best effects? This knowledge was no doubt preserved by tradition. The way the calendar works in nature is by the appearance of the stars as they are seen at sunrise or sunset. Every single day the stars appear to be in a position approximately one degree different from what they were at the same time on the day before. So the astronomer-priest is the keeper of the calendar; the man who knows the passage of the seasons and when to advise the farmers to plant their crops. This is vital knowledge and any civilization of the Stone Age type with which we are dealing must have a good agricultural organization. They were well aware that without the gods of time they had no chance of getting the maximum yield from their fields; hence the importance of the sun, stars and planets in their ritual life.

The extension of Tiahuanaco power to the coast has provided us with much more knowledge than we could have if their culture had remained in the lighlands. Up in the mountains the climate is moist, and the prospects of preserving cloth and feather work are extremely poor. So we can expect to find little around Tiahuanaco beyond the magnificent stone carving. When the Tiahuanacans invaded the coast the influence of their style of art was reflected in the habits of the indigenous people. Their burial sites from this period yield the most amazing collections of textiles and feather work. Tunics were made with patterns carefully set out in little squares of different colours; the patterns inside the squares were of alternating colours. The weavers apparently enjoyed a kind of game in which they had a black square with a yellow condor in it followed by a yellow square with a black condor; then a red square with a green condor and a green square with a red one. The variants on the theme, sometimes using as many as six different colours on six different backgrounds, are worked out to cover the whole space of the garment in a regular geometric series. It is natural that a weaver translates a drawing from curved lines to angular ones because of the right-angled criss-cross of the textile threads when weaving. But the Tiahuanaco people took the geometric construction of their designs much farther, enough to show us that this was not just a technical force of work with them but also a pleasure, and became a fashion which was enjoyed by all who wore these remarkable geometric garments.

This design element also appears on pottery. The Tiahuanaco influence on the coast encouraged Nasca potters to develop a totally different style; the quality of the pot becomes much coarser, thicker, and the shape much simpler. The design follows the Tiahuanaco angular pattern and is called epigonal. These wares show the older range of colours but simplified to a regular juxtaposition and contrast of some four different tones. Similarly we find in Tiahuanaco feather-work simple repeated patterns of very strong design, and the use of feathers from all the brilliant birds which were available on the coast.

The introduction of Tiahuanaco art to the coastal peoples must have been rather violent, because of the almost total abandonment of

Tapestry from the central coast of Peru, woven in post-Tiahuanaco times, probably the twelfth century A.D. This is woven on a simple web with pictorial sections of polychrome tapestry separated from each other by open areas. The whole has been overlaid by red tassels. Such a splendid garment was probably worn by a priest on ceremonial occasions.

A Paraccas textile fringe covered with pictorial embroidery on a plain web. This represents a divine being with a long tail wearing a tunic. His serpent-tongue ends in a small human figure. From one arm a trophy head depends; in the other hand is a bronze tumi-knife, used by warriors for decapitating their enemies. Early centuries A.D. or last centuries B.C. From the region of the Paraccas peninsula.

Far right:
Paraccas textile representing warriors disguised as magical felines. This band is in the usual Paraccas technique of overall embroidery on a plain web, which was even used for large sheets of cloth as much as twelve feet square. The colours are all natural dyes of mineral origin and astonishing permanence. These textiles have been buried in sandy graves for two thousand years. From the region of the Paraccas peninsula, last centuries B.C.

The monolithic gateway
which forms an entrance to
the courtyard known as the
Kalasassaya, at Tiahuanaco
The central figure may
represent the sun god, weep-
ing his traditional tears of
gold and carrying his lightning serpents. He is flanked
by rows of winged human
figures, all carrying staves
with condor heads. The
whole design is typical of
Tiahuanaco art, and differs
widely from the style of Inca
symbolic design. This gateway has been the subject of
many theoretical discussions
and has even been ascribed
to antediluvian times;
but the style is closely associated with all other Tia-
huanaco remains, and both
carbon 14 and sequence
datings place it after the
Nasca and Mochica cultures
of Peru, and considerably
before the Inca period. The
time-range possible is from
the sixth to the tenth centuries of the Christian era.

130

Nasca style. But, to the Tiahuanaco people, this must have been a
cultural contact of considerable value which enriched their life with
many fine products not obtainable in their mountain homeland, such
as cotton and humming-bird feathers. Also there was a production of
large scale pottery. A famous ceramic figure of a llama, now in Lima,
stands over three feet high. How the problem was solved of baking a
hollow pottery figure of this size, using only the primitive equipment
known to the Peruvians is something quite astounding. It implies
the use of local skills brought to their highest perfection for the
purposes of the religion of the conquerors from the highlands.

Why Tiahuanaco fell we have no idea. Whether it was due to a
raid from the Indians of the Amazon valley who occasionally attacked
the highlands or whether there was war with the neighbouring people
of Huari or whether it was pestilence we do not know. The downfall
was total and complete. The coastal art gradually degenerated.
Tiahuanaco style pottery in the highlands, which was always neat
and strong, thoroughly epigonal in character – became weaker and
weaker, feeble in design and bad in construction. The great empire,
even in its homeland totally shattered, left only small villages as
centres of civilization among the mountain valleys to survive for a
few centuries more. The Incas, coming down from the north, took over
the whole culture. But from Inca tradition, remains of pottery, and
a box containing Inca textiles found near Lake Titicaca it is quite

The Beginning of Civilization in Peru

clear that Tiahuanaco was regarded as a holy place and a town of pilgrimage right through the rest of Peruvian history.

We now come to the northern half of the coast of Peru, the semi-desert country north of Lima extending to the borders of Ecuador. At first, in the southern part of this region, fishing villages developed a higher culture shown by the presence of small buildings made of adobe and a development of a long series of pottery vessels. Most of these vessels have globular bodies and are fitted with a curious spout which is made like a hollow loop with a single neck at the top of it. These vessels are slightly porous, and when filled with water the porosity keeps them cool. The double neck forces one to pour, very gently, a small stream of water; any attempt to tip them up and pour out the water quickly results in an air lock in the loop and general splashing and stoppage of the main flow of water. The vessels are beautifully made. At first they were coiled, and the spouts were rolled over the fingers. This early ware was a coarse pottery, reddish or greyish in texture. In fact a lot of it seems to have been deliberately baked in holes in the ground which were covered with leaves and perhaps seaweed, so that the pottery carbonized and came out black instead of red. The first of these cultures is known as Cupisnique. It dates from the ninth century B.C. and develops quite slowly in association with simple weaving, woodwork and the building of houses. The house walls vary through time in the use of different shaped adobe bricks. Some are simply rolls of clay made up into cylinders; others were made into cones packed with their pointed ends jamming together in the centre of the walls. Later on the square block adobe technique for building developed.

After a gradual development from the coarse, strong beautifully modelled Cupisnique work, we find a series of pots which are known as Mochica wares. The Mochica people were not as interested in colour as the peoples in southern Peru, and from the first century B.C. until the end of the eighth century they were producing pottery which was covered by a cream toned slip decorated by linear designs painted in a clay containing a lot of iron oxide. This gives a rather attractive reddish brown colour which varies to deep purplish brown if fired at slightly different temperatures. Often the same pots have both colour tones of the reddish brown paint, due to differences of heating during burning. It appears that these pots were burnt in small bonfires in shallow depressions in the ground, or even in large old pots which served as temporary kilns. The modelling and drawing on the pots gives us a complete picture of life among the Mochica. We find their warriors, wearing loin cloths and quilted tunics, chasing each other with large wooden war clubs with a point at one end and a thick round head at the other. One struck one's enemy down with the head and then stabbed him with the butt of the club. They were quite terrifying weapons.

These Mochica people also developed considerable skill in casting bronze from local copper and tin ores. This was used to make very heavy copper axes, which were never hafted on a wooden handle, but slung by thick cord from the wrist so that they would be used by hand for cutting up the enemy. Thinner plates in the same form as choppers and knives were worn in the turban-like headdresses of the warriors. Great noblemen wore long gowns, and women wore simple straight gowns with a piece of embroidery at the neck. Both sexes wore turbans,

Large stone head from the ruined site of Tiahuanaco in Bolivia. The headdress is decorated with low relief carvings probably representing pumas. The treatment of the face with tear-bands depending from the eyes indicate that this may be a head of the sun god Inti, who in later Inca times was reputed to have wept tears which became the gold of earth. Now in the open-air Museum of La Paz, Bolivia

131

Above:
Lake Titicaca, the highest in the world and a jewel of beauty in the bleak and parched Altiplano. In the mythology of the region this was regarded as the birthplace of the sun and the way into the light for the first ·men.

Right:
Machu Picchu, the Inca city which was not known to exist until 1912, when it was discovered by Hiram Bingham in the gorge of the Urabamba river. The site required the provision of hundreds of stairways, all of them built with the astonishing skill and precision for which the Inca domains are famous.

The walls of Sacsahuaman, the fortress which guarded the Inca capital of Cuzco. The walls were constructed of huge fitted blocks of stone and reached a height of sixty feet. After the Conquest the Spaniards plundered the fortress for building stone.

and women wore plain earrings and did their hair in long plaits. Men wore much more elaborate earrings and were altogether more decorated with featherwork and jewellery than the women.

The Mochica ruled the northern coastal areas of Peru for some centuries. They seem to have been slightly influenced by the Huari style of art at a later period, principally in the southern region. It appears that in their earlier phases the Mochica people had several city states, and there is no very definite evidence that they were ever federated into a unified empire. It may be that they were a series of towns with similar customs, similar dress, similar religion, but remaining somewhat separate as is shown by comparatively minor differences in their artistic style.

The disruption of the old Mochica culture came from the gradual spread of control exercised over the northern half of Peru by the people of Huari, a city contemporary with Tiahuanaco and even more powerful. It also spread a strongly geometric influence on pottery, but its fall in about 800 A.D. had nothing like the same effect on local culture. It may well be that its influence during three centuries of existence was mitigated by the presence of the very ancient religious centre of Pachacamac, from where the epigonal style associated with the late periods of both Tiahuanaco and Huari radiated along the coast of Peru. Just how the three cities were politically linked is not

Far right:
A boy of the Javahé tribe wearing a necklace of glass beads and a bone lip ornament.

Right, below:
A Karajá Indian of Brazil preparing the points of arrows, watched by his son who holds a bow in his left hand. The arrows are tipped with poison which is left to dry in the sun before the arrow is used.

An Aymara Indian fisherman of Lake Titicaca. In the background are hand-coiled pottery vessels for food storage and cooking. The ever-present totora reeds are bundled for making houses as well as for binding up to make the little boats used for fishing.

known, but it is probably significant that their artistic influence failed at approximately the same period in the ninth century A.D.

On the central coast of Peru several local art styles developed, and produced in particular good metal work and fine textiles; but they were to be assimilated within little more than a century into the Chimú kingdon.

In the eleventh century there arrived on the coast a great chief and his noble followers, carried on a fleet of balsa rafts from the north. This was the arrival of the Chimú. There is an excellent legendary list of the officials who came with the Chimú chief, Naymlap. They included a chief minister, a court metal worker, keepers of records, and of course, a cup bearer for the king. These Chimú were far more advanced in metal-using techniques than their predecessors. The little evidence that survives from pottery and wood carving suggests that on the whole the new basic culture followed straight on from that of the Mochica people. The change is just the kind we should expect if the conquest was achieved by a ruling group of great power but comparatively small numbers.

The Chimú love of metalwork, particularly in silver and gold, produced a great artistic flowering in this medium and it influenced all the other arts. The most conservative, however, were the women who continued weaving their elegant geometric patterns, using little

A circular plate of gold worn as a pectoral ornament, from Ecuador, probably of the thirteenth or fourteenth century A.D. The figure combines elements of a lizard or perhaps a tree-frog and of a woman with her breasts symbolised by raised dots. The patterns of birds remind one of designs from the Peruvian coast. There is little doubt that this beautiful piece of abstraction in art was a fertility symbol, perhaps a charm for the welfare of the tribe whose chief wore it. British Museum, London.

Right:
A Quechua Indian from the northern region of Peru. The brilliant colours of his costume recall the pre-columbian cultures of Peru.

Beaten gold pendants from the Tolima region of highland Colombia, probably fourteenth or fifteenth century A.D. The figures take the basic form of human beings but the central one is a horned figure with flowers beside his mouth. In some ways it is similar in concept to the 'dontso bug' of Navajo mythology, where it is the messenger of the gods. This figure ends in a symbolic half-moon knife. British Museum.

figures to cover the entire design with repetitions but without the skill of the Tiahuanaco weavers of changing colours progressively throughout a pattern. The Chimú woven cloths are not unlike Mochica cloth of traditional designs as we find them painted on Mochica pots; but the figures often show decorations which prove their relationship to the true Chimú culture. Pottery changes completely. From the potter's point of view this was a catastrophe. Shapes become formalized, human figures become dull, puppet-like shapes on the pots, and figure-vases become rare. Nearly everything was made in a mould and wherever possible the pottery seems to have been fired in a reducing atmosphere, so that the pots come out black rather than red. However some pots are in existence which have been made from a single mould, and yet one pot is red and its fellow is black. There must have been some reason for the choice but this we do not understand in the present day.

Below, left to right:
A girl of the Maku tribe of the Japura River. A man of the Suyá tribe of the Xingú River. He wears large ear-plugs and the lip disk which denotes his married status. Boys of the Tukuna tribe off on a hunting trip. A man and a woman of the Kashin-aua tribe. The feather orna-ments come from macaws and are brilliantly coloured.

The Chimú organized their dominions, improving on the roads of Mochica times, building very much greater stepped pyramids for the service of their gods, and also erecting huge stepped constructions, mostly made of mud brick over natural rock formation, which are said to be the fortresses marking the boundary of their kingdom. The most famous of these is the Paramonga, a few miles north of Lima. The richness of Chimú culture is shown in the remains of their towns, particularly of their capital Chan Chan, which was divided into many town squares containing houses. There were open spaces within each square of buildings, some of which were especially adapted as water-gardens which irrigated the dry soil of these city blocks, and permitted the growth of beans and other family foodstuffs. The walls of the buildings were made of mud brick, adobe, and were elaborately carved into patterns which are like the Chimú textile art. These were once brilliantly coloured. However, once in a century or so

A Karajá Indian weaving a basket. The enlarged ear-lobes are to be found in many of the Amazon tribes.

rain storms occurred which caused great damage. The most recent one greatly damaged the walls of the ancient city. However, archaeologists had made drawings and photographs so that we are fully aware of the extent of these wonderfully decorated walls as they were when first excavated.

The Chimú towns were all built on the dry ground above the valleys, where the rapid little rivers came down from the mountains with their burden of silt. These water courses were carefully spread out, and artificial canals were dug to divert the water. Thus, a coastal valley was something like an irrigated oasis, always green and planted richly with cotton bushes and huge fields of maize, pepper, many varieties of beans, and pleasant fruits; life among the Chimú was possibly very comfortable indeed. The towns were built just above the cultivated area and most of them were within easy reach of roads which not only led from town to town along the coast, but also down to

139

Left to right:

Pottery figure of a man carrying a foal. It is probably a llama, one of the few animals of the South American continent suitable for domestication. Chimú culture.

Pottery vessel of the Recuay culture of highland Peru. The figures represent a priest often shown on Recuay vases as a llama breeder – in the clutches of a gigantic puma which may represent the terrible powers of nature. The jaguar skin and the tunic of the priest have been produced by a wax-resistant dyeing technique akin to batik. Eighth to tenth centuries A.D.

Nasca vase representing the head of a decapitated enemy. The cheeks are painted with designs symbolising hawks. The headdress is a cane cap wrapped with textile and edged with humming birds. The colours are all polychrome clay slips painted on before firing. Such trophy heads have been found in graves; they are not shrunk like the more recent Jivaro trophy heads but probably served the same purpose as testimony to the bravery of a warrior. Probably about the fourth century A.D. from the southern coast of Peru.

A Mochica mythological vase, probably sixth century A.D. Painted in red over cream slip, this elaborate piece of work depicts divine beings in the form of a longtusked mountain god who wears puma heads as ear ornaments, approached by a spider-man with a similar mask on his back. Whether the spider-man is a priest in ceremonial costume approaching an unheeding divinity, or whether he is simply a character in a myth is unknown to us. National Museum, Lima.

Left:
Portraiture among the
Mochica; probably of the
sixth or seventh century A.D.
All these beautifully modelled vases have been burn-
ished, covered with cream
slip and then painted with an
iron oxide pigment before
firing. They show the development of true portraiture
during a relatively short
period, from the warrior on
the right to the perfection of
the flautist on the left, which
alone of the three has been
treated with true realism,
including an approach to
showing skin texture. In the
centre is a Mochica potter,
using a spatula for working
over the surface of a vase
with a portrait face. Note the
decorated ear ornaments,
and the use of formal face-
painting. The warrior, in
rather more stylised technique, is possibly the earliest
in the series, though the
burnishing of the surface has
been skilfully accomplished.
He is armed with a short
club, a circular shield,
conical helmet and quilted
tunic and loin cloth.
British Museum.

Guarani Indians
of modern Paraguay.

good beaches whence the fishing boats could go out to bring in sea food just as required.

The Chimú had already inherited a civilization, which they developed beyond Mochica traditions. Altogether they produced a rich and comfortable civilization. Their chief god was Sí, who was the moon spirit. To these dwellers in the hot coastal lands the sun was a terrifying creature – one did not go out in the noonday for fear of sun-stroke – a very reasonable fear – and, of course, exposures to the dry air and the hot sun could cause a great deal of physical damage. So the cool evenings, especially on those nights when the moon gave sufficient illumination, were considered the happiest and best periods for fishing, hunting and even weaving. At such times the beneficient moon god brought cool waters and good food for the populace.

Chimú dress was very like the Mochica; men wore rather more elaborate headdresses, the greater nobles glittered with jewellery both in gold and silver, and their households were rich in drinking vessels and gold plate. They seem to have led very ordered lives, rich and reasonably peaceful because they were able to defend their borders against all comers. This was possible through their good organization and plentiful supplies of metal for making weapons.

Their worship of the gods was sometimes highly erotic and in some of the spring festivals the young people of the towns enjoyed a kind of sports day in which the final event was a mass race in which everybody was completely naked. The runners made for the temple pyramid of the moon god. After racing up the stairway ascending from one platform to another, the first boy and girl who reached the very top had sexual intercourse before the God and before the people, in the hopes of bringing fertility to the fields and richness to the ocean. This kind of thing would, of course, have shocked the comparatively puritan Incas up in their highlands. But in the earlier period of Chimú power there was only slight trading contact between these people of the hot coast land and the tribes of the high mountains.

142

The Inca Power

The Incas, according to their own story, appeared in highland Peru in the eleventh century. The story, recorded after the Spanish conquest, has many variants, some versions say that they came from the south, and one makes it clear that the author thought the Incas were descendants of the ancient rulers of Tiahuanaco. However, other stories bring the Inca family from the forests and great rivers of the Amazon valley. The legend recounts how a group of four of his children were sent out by the sun god. Their leader, the Inca Manco, carried a wedge of gold. He and his sister Mama Ocllo, were instructed to carry this with them, to put it on the ground every night before they made their camp. Eventually the golden wedge would sink into the ground at a place which was the very centre of the earth. There the Inca family were to found a city which in due time would dominate the four quarters of the world.

On their way through Peru the brothers of the first Inca were changed into mysterious protective beings; one into a condor, another into a great puma, another into a sacred white llama; but the Inca Manco and Mama Ocllo continued the journey. One day they reached a small town on the slopes of a mountain valley. As soon as they came to the lower reaches of this town, across the Apurimac river, they put down their golden wedge. It sank rapidly into the earth and disappeared from view. This they knew was to be the sign that they had reached the Cuzco – the navel, or the centre of the earth. It was destined to be the home of their family from which they were to rule the future empire of Tahuantinsuyu – The Place of the Four Directions – in other words, all the known world.

For two generations the Inca family ruled only the lower half of the city of Cuzco; the third generation took over the whole town and parts of the river valley nearby. By then the growing group of people ruled by the Inca family showed enough progress to rouse the envious anger of the powerful Chanca confederation of tribes. War was declared; the reigning Inca, a young man, went into battle and was terrified of the great armies confronting him. Because his army was defeated and retreated on Cuzco, he was deposed and executed. His name was Yahuarhuaccac which means 'One who Weeps Blood'. In their dire straits the Inca nobles ceremonially named his successor after the great creator god Viracocha, the great being beyond the earth and the sky, the Great Power Above. He was worshipped only in

The monolithic Intihuatana
in the Inca city of Machu
Picchu. The 'tethering post
of the Sun' was a sacred
place in each Inca city. It
was used for measuring the
shadow cast by the raised
pillar at noon. Thus it was
possible to give the day of the
return of the sun from its
mid-winter position in the
north after its passage over-
head and on to its southward
limit. Such Intihuatanas
determined the sequence of
festivals for the sun ritual.
Fifteenth century.

144

a single temple some fifteen miles from Cuzco; otherwise it was thought that he was present in the heart of every human being and in the centre of every human habitation. To name their Sapa Inca for Viracocha was both an appeal and an assertion that they were under divine protection. They now claimed the blessing of the supreme creator, someone even greater than their own father sun god, Inti. Sapa Inca Viracocha was in fact a brilliant man. He reorganized his defence forces, surrounded groups of the enemy by making extremely risky marches across the mountains, and finally succeeded in defeating the whole of the great Chanca confederacy. He had now established a highland domain of perhaps only two or three hundred square miles, but still it was a united kingdom that respected the Inca as being the Sapa Inca – or the only Inca – as its supreme ruler. He set about organizing a social structure for the new nation.

There can be no doubt that the Inca social system, the construction of roads, the organization of towns, and the keeping of records by means of mnemonic devices of knotted strings called *quipus*, were all in existence among the tribal states of the highlands before Inca Viracocha took over his hard-won kingdom. His genius lay in organizing the whole system for the single purpose of maintaining unity; of bringing the whole of his domain into a single organized Inca culture.

The result was a superbly *ordered* society. People from each separate town in the kingdom wore slightly different dresses so that the Inca's intelligence service could tell immediately who was visiting whom, or if there was any risk of a conspiracy against his rule. He established store-houses so that if there was any shortage in one part of his empire the Inca could immediately supply relief.

Portrait head of the third or fourth century A.D., from a Mochica period vessel. This represents a prisoner with a rope round his neck. If the opening of the vase was deliberately made to resemble a headdress he would have come from the highland regions. The other picture makes an interesting comparison with the Mochica portrait. It shows a Quechua-speaking man from highland Peru, actually from the Cuzco region, and plainly of the same race. Note the embroidered poncho which though woven very recently continues the ancient traditions of Peruvian textile art.

Part of the great city of the Chimú, Chan Chan, the ruins of which spread across eleven square miles of the desert near Trujillo in Peru.

He established other depots of food and clothing which were kept for the service of the sun god. Thus, the Inca took one third of the produce of the land, the sun god one third and the farmers themselves kept one third. If it was necessary for the army to march anywhere, the store-rooms of the Inca were used. If there was a pestilence, a drought or any suffering sent from the gods, the store-rooms of the sun god supplied the wants of the people. Thus the farmers paid their tribute as a kind of insurance.

With human society guarded and protected against natural accidents the Inca kingdom became very successful. Its centralized organization made it into a powerful unity which was destined to spread its wings over the whole of the area of Peru. This was a most fantastic empire at its zenith, being some 2,000 miles in length from north to south, and at its widest part from the coast to the point where the Andes dipped down into the tropical jungle, some 500 miles across. This Empire of the Four Quarters became an enormous organization traversed by three great high roads; a coastal road and one road along each slope of the Cordillera of the Andes. The road furthest to the east ran along the Andes just above the level of the forest and parts of it are now only just beginning to come to the light of scientific knowledge as excavation and the clearing of forests for agriculture uncover remains of this third of the great roads of the Inca.

The Inca system of roads was basic to their economy. As new areas were added to the empire, communications were pushed forward so that in case of tribal uprisings the Inca armies could arrive quickly.

146

The Inca Power

But a much more important function of the roads was as the means of distribution of goods and services and the carrying of intelligence to the Inca and his administrators. The very fact of good roads and good communications was the reason why many smaller tribal groups opted, of their own free will, to join the Inca civilization. The ancient coast road, which was improved by the Inca, was marked among the shifting sands by rows of large tree trunks which acted as guide posts. After any particularly violent storm, when the desert sands were blown over the road, these posts marked the way for the Chimu population to clear away the obstructions and to prepare a new hard surface. In the highlands the roads were constructed in the face of the most enormous physical difficulties. They were sometimes cut into the steep sloping sides of mountains, sometimes tunnelled through overhanging buttresses of rocks and sometimes taken across ravines by means of suspension bridges.

These bridges were basically two enormous cables of plaited osiers hung side by side across a ravine and anchored firmly to massive stone stanchions. After the cables had been dragged into place, a layer of planks was strapped across; then smaller cables were put on either side above them. From the smaller cables ropes were laced underneath the two main cables and served as an extra support at the sides of the footway, and also made a handrail for travellers. Thus the bridge, sometimes a hundred feet or more in length, was suspended over ravines in such a way that one trotted down a slope and then up the curving track to the farther end of the bridge and the continuation of the road. The bridges could sway freely in any wind; in damp weather they expanded somewhat and the downward curve became steeper; in the dry weather they shrank and were less steep. The whole thing was flexible and adjustable and, therefore, reasonably safe. Repair was entrusted to the nearby villages and small towns. Special overseers were appointed to examine the bridge daily and when any of the cables showed signs of fraying the organization immediately sprang into action and new cables were made and replaced the old.

The constant security and survey service on the roads maintained Inca communications throughout their empire. On the rock-cut part of the roads a look-out was kept for damage caused by occasional avalanches and rock slides. If the volume of these caused damage beyond the capacity of the local community to repair, a message was sent to a nearby town. Then the army garrison was sent into immediate action, breaking away rock, clearing a path, and if necessary cutting a new line of road. The cutting was done by means of wooden wedges which were driven into cracks of the rocks and then soaked with water so that the natural expansion of the wedge caused the rock to crack further and allowed it to be pried loose with bronze tipped levers. If it was difficult to find any cracks to open in this way a bonfire was lit on the piece of rock that it was desired to move. When the red hot ashes were cleared away, the hot surface underneath was doused with cold water so as to produce a sudden shattering action which usually opened up the necessary fissures.

Every town and village in the empire had its portion of uncultivable high country for the breeding of llamas and the preservation of wild guanaco. This ensured supplies of meat and of fine wool. Land for growing maize and beans, together with whatever pumpkin

Pelicans in clay, from a carved adobe wall in Chan Chan. The clay was built up in blocks of well-mixed material, smoothed down and then carved. Probably fifteenth century A.D.

vines and other food plants were available was cleared on nearby slopes. When the slopes were very steep they were lined with walls, placed almost vertically above one another like the risers of gigantic stairways. Between the walls earth was piled up. Sometimes it was scraped from the hillsides, sometimes brought from a distance in carrying baskets and just thrown into the narrow spaces between the walls on the steep slopes. The result was landscaping which appears very like the hillside vineyards of central Europe. Steep paths led from one level to another and each level had a little stream of water carefully led along it by diverting the mountain streams and making them run into channels. Householders responsible for particular strips of land had their water supply allocated in regular rotation. After half a day of water flowing through their trenches, they opened a sluice at the end of their field which allowed the water to pass on and be used for irrigating the next field. After one row of fields had been dealt with the stream was released to plunge down the mountain side and then run along the next row. Thus there was a regular supply of water everywhere. Access to the fields was made comparatively easy by the staircases which ran from one level to another. In this way whole hillsides were covered by terraces. These were known as Andenes and it is from this remarkable feature of Inca agricultural organization that the whole range of mountains, the Andes, has taken its name.

The Inca military system was basically one of conscription. Army commanders were usually members of the Inca family but young men of promise were able to earn promotion, and might indeed become commanders of one of the great army corps of Peru. In this case, they were usually married to princesses of Inca descent and so absorbed into the family hierarchy. For the ordinary young man military service lasted anything from half a year to five years according to circumstances. Those who were most capable as fighting men were specially trained. Other less active individuals were organized for the military commissariat. Their function was to carry supplies of food, arms and clothing for the main body of warriors and also to act as an

Below, left:
A wooden kero, or vase for pouring libations. The puma head and the style of decoration are typically late Inca in style, though it is now believed that these vessels were made after the Spanish conquest. The surface has been laquered with coloured mastic.

Below:
A golden mask for a Chimú mummy pack from the north Peruvian coast. The headdress, an ornament originally worn in the hair, represents a warrior's axe-blade with decorations in the form of puma heads. The nose clip and ear pendants were customary wear for important men in the Chimú kingdom. Thirteenth century A.D. Collection of Señor Mujica Gallo.

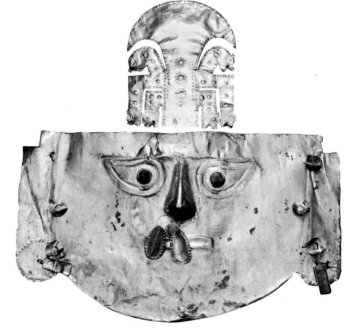

organized labour corps. They threw up earthworks when necessary, extended the road system, built bridges, and made the general transport of forces quicker and more easy than would otherwise have been possible. On the coast army supplies were occasionally taken on fleets of balsa rafts which sailed along parallel to the coast road and deposited supplies at storage points ready for the army's use whenever needed.

The campaign of the Incas against the Chimú came only about sixty years before the Spanish invasion. There was very bitter fighting, since the Chimú were not anxious to submit to strangers from the highlands who would take away their golden ornaments for the greater glory of the sun god. There was also social distress since the Chimú very well knew that their free social organization would break down under the impact of Inca puritan morality; it was made perfectly clear to them that the Inca disapproved of their general way of life. However, after a great battle in which the Inca troops stormed the Paramonga fortress there was no possibility of further resistance. The Chimú kingdom made a graceful submission, and the Incas, not wishing to face another great war, accepted the position and appointed Inca governors in all the Chimú towns. They commanded that a temple of the sun god should be placed in front of each of the temples to the Chimú's moon god Sí, and took away all available golden ornaments to form the decoration of the Temple of the Sun at Cuzco. Apart from this the Chimú were supposed to live their own life farming and fishing, building new town blocks, decorating the houses in their own way, and producing their fine

The most typical of all Inca pottery forms, the so called aryballus. Vessels of this shape range from six inches to three feet in height. The tiny loops at the lip were used for securing a cover to protect the contents. The larger pots of this kind were carried on the back, by a thong which passed as a broad band across the forehead of the carrier. The thong then passed down through one handle on the body of the vase, over the modelled nub on the back, down through the other loop handle and thence up to the forehead band. In this way great weights could be carried by the sure-footed porters of Inca times. Kemper Collection.

An embossed gold plate, perhaps the front of a ceremonial ear ornament. The central figure is the earth goddess and around her are symbols of various plants; maize, yucca, and sweet potato. The most prominent symbol is a sea shell, which is held in the hands of the surrounding figures and forms a major part of the design. Such shells have been found in Chimu graves, where they were used as jewel containers. It has been suggested that this disc represents an agricultural calendar, and the appearance of a solemn dance in the circle of figures may be the expression of a sequence of time. Mujico Gallo Collection, Lima.

149

IDOLOS
DELOS INGAS
INTI VANACAVRITA
BOTO CO

CAPITVLODELOSIDOLOS
VACABILLCAINCAP

Above:
The Inca and his queen paying homage to the origins of the royal house. Drawing made a generation after the conquest of Peru by Don Felipe Huaman Poma de Ayala, a mestizo of Inca descent, during the time he spent in Spain. The manuscript is now in the Royal Library of Copenhagen.

Above, right:
The Sapa Inca with his idols. These are often, as in the case of the Kenko stone, natural rocks. The Kenko is shown at the top of the mountain with the name of the hero Huanacauri who was supposed to have been replaced by the rock. All members of his family might wear the golden earrings and the deep belt of fine embroidery, but the Sapa Inca alone might wear the borla, the diadem of red wool surmounted by the sacred feathers. From the manuscript of Huaman Poma de Ayala.

weaving of cotton goods not only for themselves but also for supplying the Incas in the highlands. Their sexual behaviour was the subject of new 'instructions' which appear in the form of a series of particularly ugly and primitive black pottery vessels which instructed the ordinary Chimú householder in the simplicities of sexual intercourse according to the Inca code. However, the brilliance of Chimú civilization remained intact in most ways. Their silver work was particularly fine right to the end of the Inca empire.

After the capture of the Chimú lands, the expansion of the Inca empire of Tahuantinsuyu accelerated. The great Emperor Topa Inca Yupanqui was not only a leader of his country in the fields of arts and sciences, but was also famous for the diligence with which he visited every town within the empire to make sure that the laws were properly administered and that people received fair treatment from the appointed governors. His laws were of the ancient Inca pattern and very severe. Imprisonment was not used as a punishment, but an offender was likely to suffer mutilation. People had hands, ears, lips or feet cut off according to their crime. Their wounds were then healed and they were given both food and clothing from public store; but they were forced to sit at the entrance of towns so that all visitors and strangers coming there would note the severity of the Inca penal system and act accordingly.

During the reign of this great Inca there had been an invasion of the southern coast by a group of people from Argentina, the Calchaqui. This possible danger induced him to send the Inca armies on a tremendous journey which took them as far as the River Maule in

150

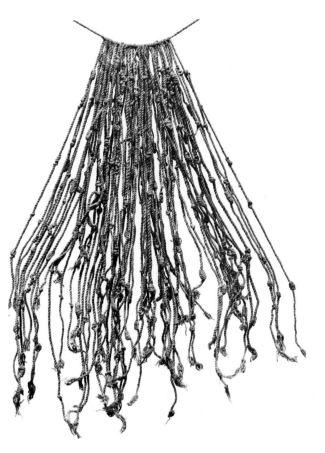

Chile. They consolidated the Inca empire this far south, extending both the coast and the highland roads and pacifying the tribes on the way. Occasionally, in the high Andes even in modern times people find the dried and mummified bodies of Inca officials who had died during this campaign. They include the widely publicized discovery of the mummy of a little princess who was found wrapped in her beautiful textile garments secured by silver pins, in 1965.

Once the southern part of the empire was secure, the Inca was free to study the possibilities of expansion to the north. Already the Cara of Ecuador had learnt sufficiently of Inca ways to build themselves greater fortresses, to train armies, and to bring many of their social customs into line with the Inca style of organization. It was apparent that here might be another rival power. But Inca Topa Yupanqui did not live to complete this work.

In a period of peace, however, he made a most remarkable expedition into the Pacific. With a fleet of balsa rafts he sailed to some distant islands and returned after four months, bringing with him some dark-skinned people with curly hair, strange wood carvings, and supplies of food of kinds which were not known in Peru. It seems that in this voyage he may have reached the Taumotu or the Marquesas Islands. However, the journeys on the great ocean only showed that there was no country to be found which was worth bringing into the folds of Tahuantinsuyu, so this Inca expedition into the ocean was not followed up. Similarly with the great forests of the Amazon Basin; the Inca armies patrolled the borderlands, occasionally fighting back raiding parties of the wild forest Indians

Above, left:
The Sapa Inca examines his storehouses, and receives a full reckoning from his Quipucamayoc. From the manuscript of Huaman Poma de Ayala.

Above:
An ancient Peruvian quipu. These devices were used for keeping records, and to some extent they seem to have been a substitute for the written word. The colour is said to have indicated the subject dealt with on the knots. Each string has knots made with differing numbers of turns of the cord; these are decimals varying from one to ten. The knots nearest the carrying string are the units, below them come the tens, the third line is hundreds, and the fourth thousands. For modern scholars these knotted documents remain indecipherable, with the exception of a few which have been found to contain astronomical calculations. Fourteenth or fifteenth century A.D.

151

and more often organizing trade in feathers and furs, in exchange for pottery and weapons from the highlands. But it was realized that people from the highlands could not live in the conditions of the tropical forests for any length of time, and so no serious attempt was made to expand the empire in that direction.

When Topa Inca Yupanqui died his son Huayna Ccapac became Sapa Inca. He was one of the wisest of the Inca family and spent a great deal of time in codifying the laws and strengthening the internal communications of his country. Eventually he found it necessary to organize the inclusion of the Cara kingdom of Quito within the empire. The Cara warriors were fierce and brave, but the conquest was a comparatively short campaign in which a numerically superior army was able to surround the local fortresses and deal with them one by one. The Cara chief, the Scyri of Quito, surrendered and his country was formally brought into Tahuantinsuyu.

The conquered chief had a very beautiful daughter, and when peace was made she became one of the junior wives of the Sapa Inca. But this happy marriage which was really, it appears, a true love match, resulted in the final end of the Inca Empire. The Sapa Inca had a son, Huascar, by his Ccoya or senior wife, who was thus destined to be the next Sapa Inca. He also had a son by the beautiful princess from Quito. During his lifetime the two young men, together with many other

An example of the highly efficient organisation which lay behind the social structure of the Incas. Terraces such as these were constructed near every Inca city; the soil was conserved in them and even in the extraordinary conditions of the Andes the populace could be self-supporting. The one shown here lies near the road—cut out of solid rock—to the capital city of Cuzco.

The Inca Power

brothers and sisters from the great harem of the Sapa Inca, were educated together.

On the death of Huayna Ccapac it was revealed that he wished to divide the kingdom. The old Inca dominion of Tahuantinsuyu was to go to the Sapa Inca Huascar and the Cara kingdom was to be inherited as a separate Inca domain by the son of Huayna Ccapac and the princess from Quito. This young man was named Atahuallpa. He was brave, intelligent, a wonderful organizer and tremendously ambitious. It was clear to him that he was more capable than his 'divine' brother, so he intrigued first and then organized a Cara army of his own under two brilliant generals to make an attack on his brother's forces. Little by little he drove southwards. The Inca army was unable to resist, being first attacked from one side and then from the other, as the two Cara armies moved southwards. Eventually Cuzco itself was abandoned by the Inca and very shortly afterwards he was captured by his halfbrother. It was then that Atahuallpa was self-inducted as the Sapa Inca and he proceeded to rule over Peru. The true Inca was kept in his palace–a prisoner in a room of stone.

Shortly after this, news came to Cuzco of strange people landing on the coast; they came in great boats with white wings like birds; they were white-faced and wore black beards; many of them wore grey stone which could not be pierced by darts or clubs. Some of them jumped on to the backs of gigantic llamas which galloped towards the Peruvian soldiers, and then the riders pierced them with sharp pointed spears. Indeed some of these strange creatures from out of the sea carried short tubes which discharged thunder and lightning and killed people with stone thunderbolts. These first reports suggested that the strangers were sent by the god Viracocha to seize Peru from the unlawful usurper but for some months nothing happened. In fact Pizarro and his Spanish army were obtaining reinforcements from Panama. His strengthened forces then proceeded along the coast road, receiving the surrender of town after town without any struggle. The Spaniards were given offerings of food, and housed in comfortable quarters, reserved normally for Inca officials.

After some months the invaders heard that the Inca was approaching at the head of an enormous army. They turned inland hoping to meet him in some advantageous position where at least they could discuss arrangements for placing Spanish governors over the coastal

Details of a wall in Cuzco, the Inca capital. This shows the meticulous way in which heavy blocks of hard rock were cut and fitted together. The bevelled edges to each joint added to the decorative aspect, and largely concealed the remarkable accuracy of the fit. Sometimes surface irregularities were preserved in order to give a better total quality to the wall. Sixteenth century A.D.

Pachacamac, the Lord of Life, or He who Animates the Earth, the creator god of the ancient Peruvians. This piece of woven fabric comes from a grave on the Peruvian coast, near the ruined temple of Pachacamac. The god is shown as Lord of the Creatures in the Sea, surrounded by birds and fish. The face of the deity was a deep blue, symbol of the unknown power in the depths. A late Chimú tapestry, fourteenth or fifteenth century A.D. British Museum.

provinces, which they considered they had conquered. However Atahuallpa came very slowly, stopping at various rest houses and hot baths on his way to Cajamarca. It was in this heavily defended, walled town that the Spaniards met the Inca army. They realized at a glance that they were outnumbered – about 1,000 to 1 – and they would have no chance in a fight. As they advanced Pizarro was informed that the Inca, together with his principal nobles, was to meet him in an enclosed court yard of strongly built stone houses, and the Spanish commanders placed arquebusiers and crossbowmen on the roofs of these. When the Inca at last advanced to meet them in a golden palanquin carried on the shoulders of the great nobles of his empire, the Spaniards suddenly shouted their war cry and charged straight into the mass of the Indian noblemen. They cut them down right and left, surrounded the Inca and made him a prisoner while the crossbowmen and the arquebusiers kept up a fire which paralysed the rest of the Peruvian army.

No move was made to rescue the Inca, because although he was a sacred being to his own forces, to the rest of the Peruvians he was a traitor and usurper. Unfortunately the true Inca was not able to take over the throne or to deal with the Spaniards, because his half brother had had him strangled as soon as he heard of the landing of the strangers. Thus Peru, without its divinely descended Inca to lead it, fell easily into the hands of the foreign invaders, and the glories of the Inca empire came to an unhappy end. Most of the gold extorted by the Spaniards from the Inca family and wrenched from the walls of the great Temple of the Sun in Cuzco was melted down into small ingots and sent over to Spain; very little of the Inca treasure retained its old form. The country became part of a late medieval Spanish colonial system which had almost no reference to the former organization of the Inca empire.

In Cuzco today little remains of the proud capital of the Incas. The great temples and nobles' palaces can only be recalled in the magnificent, indestructible walls which now support churches, dwellings and administrative buildings.

Conclusion

We have seen the double-continent of the Americas in a short outline, noted its fascinating variety in art and culture, and discovered that the growth from Stone Age tribe to Bronze Age empire was a natural development. It is possible that ships from the west might have been blown into the Caribbean from the time, probably in the eighteenth century B.C. when Cretan boats first entered the Atlantic. Certainly two Roman clay heads have been found in Mexico in a sound archaeological context. There are various scraps of evidence which show the probability of Norse contacts from Greenland as far south as Massachusetts Bay. There is a possibility that West African traders had sighted Brazil as early as the eleventh century. The Marquesan Islanders of the Pacific have a legend of a visit to the land of Tefiti, which seems to be twelfth-century Peru. Possibly Chinese fishermen, and Japanese also, drifted along the west coast of North America. These have all been people with fine ocean-going ships. But it remains true that not one of them had any great influence upon the life and customs of the American Indians. Maybe a tale about elephants in eastern Canadian folk-lore came from a Norse original, maybe some medieval sailor showed the Indians how to wear leggings suspended from a belt; but no one taught them how to write a single syllable either in Egyptian, Chinese, or even a letter in Phoenician, Latin or Runic. No one taught them how to use a wheel. No one introduced wheat or barley. No one persuaded them to make a plank-built boat. Thus America might really have been a New World.

American Indian culture was a self-created thing. In comparing its manifestation with the developments of civilization in the old world we find many interesting parallels. But they develop at such a different rate in America from their evolution in the old world that there is no likelihood of cross-cultural exchange of the least importance. The parallelism is best explained by the natural human reactions to the necessities of communal life. Hunters and primitive farmers have only one type of reaction to existence. They must make tools and act as nature dictates.

Much remains to be done in the investigation of the world of the American Indian. Yet even now, after less than a century of concentrated research, a general picture emerges of people developing their own civilization in a world conditioned by natural resources more than by the ingenuity of man.

Further Reading List

The following books are of recent date and all have very complete bibliographies. They are not only important in their own right, they will in turn introduce the student to still further sources of information about American antiquities.

Anders, Ferdinand. *Pantheon der Maya* Akademische Druck und Verlagsanstalt, Graz. 1963
Burland, C. A. *Magic Books from Mexico* Penguin Books, Harmondsworth. 1953
    Men without Machines Aldus Books, London. 1965
    The Gods of Mexico Eyre & Spottiswoode, London. 1966
    North American Indian Mythology Paul Hamlyn, Feltham. 1966
    The Ancient Maya Weidenfeld & Nicholson, London. 1967
    Peru under the Incas Evans Bros., London. 1968
Bushnell, G. H. S. *The Ancient Arts of the Americas* Thames & Hudson, London. 1965
Dockstader, F. J. *The Indian Art of Central America* Cory Adams & Mackay, London. 1964
    South American Indian Art Studio Vista, London. 1967
Fernandez, J. *Mexican Art* Paul Hamlyn, Feltham. 1968
Haberland, W. *North America* Methuen, London. 1968
Hagen, V. W. von. *The Desert Kingdoms of Peru* Weidenfeld & Nicolson, London. 1965
Hawgood, J. A. *The American West* Eyre & Spottiswoode, London. 1967
Huxley, M. and Capa, C. *Farewell to Eden* Chatto & Windus, London. 1965
Hyams, E. and Ordish, G. *The Last of the Incas* Longmans, London. 1963
Kubler, G. *Art and Architecture of Ancient America* Penguin Books, Harmondsworth. 1962
Lanning, E. P. *Peru before the Incas* Spectrum Books, Englewood Cliffs. 1967
Lothrop, S. K. *Treasures of Ancient America* Skira, Geneva. 1964
Mason, J. Alden. *The Ancient Civilisations of Peru* Penguin Books, Harmondsworth. 1957
Miles, C. *Indian and Eskimo artefacts of North America* Henry Regnery Co., Chicago. 1963
Moser, B. and Taylor, D. *The Cocaine Eaters* Longmans, London. 1965
Nicholson, Irene. *Mexican and Central American Mythology* Paul Hamlyn, Feltham. 1967
Soustelle, J. *Daily Life of the Aztecs* Penguin Books, Harmondsworth. 1961
Thompson, J. E. S. *The Rise and Fall of Maya Civilisation* Gollancz, London. 1956
Vaillant, G. C. (Revised by S. B. Vaillant) *The Aztecs of Mexico* Penguin Books, Harmondsworth. 1952

Acknowledgments

Black and White:
Inside front flap: J. C. Spahni. Front endpapers: Harald Schultz. Frontispiece, 10, 12: Mike Andrews. 12-13: U.S. Information Service. 13: Paul Hamlyn Library. 14 top: Museum of Primitive Art, New York. 14 bottom: I.N.A.H., Mexico City. 15: British Museum. 16, 16-17, 17: Michael Holford – Paul Hamlyn Library. 21: British Museum. 24: Michael Holford – Paul Hamlyn Library. 25 top: Royal Scottish Museum. 25 bottom: City of Birmingham Museum. 28: McCord Museum, McGill University. 29: British Museum. 32: Smithsonian Institution. 34 top and bottom, 36: Paul Hamlyn Library. 37 left: Smithsonian Institution. 37 right: Mansell Collection. 38 top: British Museum. 38 bottom: Radio Times Hulton Picture Library. 39: van Rensslaer Collection. 42 top: Axel Poignant. 40 bottom (all), 42: British Museum. 43: Museum of Primitive Art, New York. 45: Museo Nacional de Antropologia, Mexico City. 46: Henri Stierlin. 47 left: Pierre Verger – Mansell. 47 right: Eugen Kusch. 48: Irmgard Groth-Kimball. 50: Henri Stierlin. 51 top: American Museum of Natural History. 51 bottom: Giraudon. 54: Eugen Kusch. 55: Ferdinand Anton. 59 top: Roger-Viollet. 59 bottom: Henri Stierlin. 62, 63: Dumbarton Oaks. 66: Henri Stierlin. 67 top: British Museum. 67 bottom: Giraudon. 68 top: Eugen Kusch. 68 bottom: Giraudon. 70 top: Eugen Kusch. 70 bottom: I.N.A.H., Mexico City. 71: Württ. Landesmuseum, Stuttgart. 72 left: Guido Sansoni. 72 right, 73 left: Larousse. 73 right: Guido Sansoni. 74 top: British Museum. 74 bottom: Irmgard Groth-Kimball. 75: Museum of the American Indian. 76: Guido Sansoni. 77: I.N.A.H., Mexico City. 78: Ferdinand Anton. 78-79: Bodleian Library, Oxford. 81: Guido Sansoni. 82: City of Liverpool Museums. 84 top: British Museum. 84 bottom: Ferdinand Anton. 86, 88 left: British Museum. 88 right: Roger-Viollet. 90-91: Henri Stierlin. 92, 93, 95, 96, 97: Ferdinand Anton. 100: Eugen Kusch. 101, 104 bottom left and right, upper left: British Museum. 104 upper right: Cleveland Museum of Art. 108: British Museum. 112, 113: Harald Schultz. 114, 115: British Museum. 116: Dumbarton Oaks. 117, 119, 120 top: British Museum. 120 bottom: Michael Holford – Paul Hamlyn Library. 121: British Museum. 122 top: Paul Hamlyn Library. 122 bottom: Mike Andrews. 123 top: Michael Holford – Paul Hamlyn Library. 123 bottom: Mike Andrews. 124: Michael Holford – Paul Hamlyn Library. 125: Dumbarton Oaks. 126: M. Desjardins – *Realités*. 127: Paul Hamlyn Library. 130 top: Ferdinand Anton. 130 bottom, 131, 134: J. C. Spahni. 135, 138, 139: Harald Schultz. 142: Paul Almasy. 145: J. C. Spahni.

Index

Figures in italics refer to illustrations
Adobe 41, 47, 58, 131, 138
Agriculture 18, 19, 33-44, *see also particular tribes*
Alacaluf 15
Alaska 11; Indians of 21
Altiplano *126*
Amazon area 11, 35, 109, 112, 143, 151; Indians of *106*, 112, 130
American Indian 8, 14, 43, 45, 48, 121
Andenes 148
Andes 11, 35, 41, 115, 146
Apoala 68
Appalachians 39
Apurimac river 143
Argentina 35, 41, 150
Aryballus *149*
Atahuallpa 153, 154
Aymara Indian *134*
Azcapotzalco 62
Aztec 8, 51, 54, 58, 62, 65-6, 67, 69, *81*; calendar of fate 71-3, *72*; carving *70, 71, 74, 84*; clothing 75, 76, *76*; craftsmen 82-3; cruelty 79-80; daily life 75-6; festivals 75; government 69-70; Great Fast 72; law 76-80; magic 71; merchants 81-2; military training 80; New Fire *73*; pottery *84*; power 69-84; religion 73-5; sculpture *56*; writing 83

Bacabs 101
Bahamas 114
Baktun 100
Beagle Channel *12*
Bering Straits 13
Bimilek vase *74*
Bison *12-3*, 14
Bochica 116, *122*
Bogotá 116, 117
Bolas 18
Bonampak 93
Botocudo Indians 15-8, *16-7*
Brazil 109, 114; Eastern 11, 15

Bringing out of Banners 74
British Columbia, Indians of 21
Bronze Age 30, 155
Buffalo *12-3*, 36

Cajamarca 154
Calchaqui 41, 150
Caliche 45
California 35; Indians of 14; knife *15*
Canada 11
Canoes: dugout 21, *24, 29, 36*; mahogany or ceiba 93
Cara 117, 151-3
Caribs 114
Carribales 114
Ccoya 152
Central America 19
Chac 96
Chacmuls 96
Chalchihuitlicue 74
Chanca 143, 145
Chan Chan 138, *146*; carving *146*
Chavín 120, 121, 126, 127; carving *123*; temple 120
Cherokee 40
Chibcha art *122*
Chibcha-speaking tribes 109, 116
Chich'en Itzá 63, 95, 96, *96-7*
Chichimeca 78
Chicozapote wood 104
Chilan Balam 103
Chile 41, 151
Chimú 135, 142, 147, 148, 150; goldwork *110, 148, 149*; pottery 138, *140*
Ciboney 112
Cloud People 66-8
Coatlicue 77
Cocomes 95
Cocom family 96
Codex: Borbonicus 72, 73; Dresdensis 97; Egerton 2895 67; Fejervary-Mayer 82; Mendoza 78-9; Peresianus 97; Troano-Cortesianus 100, 101; Vindobonensis 62, 67; Zouche-Nuttall 68

Colhuacan 65
Colla people 127
Colombia 11, 109, 115, 116, 117; goldwork *136*
Columbus, Christopher 71, 93
Cook, Captain 21
Cordillera 11, 117, 146
Cortez, Hernando 67
Costa Rica 109, 114
Cotzumahualpan stone carving *47*
Coxcoxtli 65
Cuba 112
Cupisnique culture 131
Cuzco 127, 143, 145, 149, 153, 154,. *154*

Delaware Indian 39
Diaguita 41
Dual Lord, the 73

Earth-Mother *40, 76, 77*, 120
Ecuador 115, 117, 126, 131, 151; goldwork *136*
Eight Deer Ocelot Claw 51, 67, 68
El Dorado 116
Empire of the Four Quarters 146
Eskimos 9, 15; art *14*; carving *13*
Esmeraldas pottery *120*
Fire God 73
Flaked stone industry 14, *15*
Florida 109, 114; Indians *34, 42*; Indian warrior *18-9*; Indian Indian women 18
Fuegians 35
Gateway of the Sun 127
God: of the Breath of Life 58; of the Morning Star 71; of the Winds 63
Great Lake of Mexico 65, 74
Great Lakes 11, 35
Great Plains 13, 18, 36
Great Speaker 69
Guanaco 15, 18, 147
Guarani Indians *142*
Guatavita 116
Guatemala 58, 62, 81, 84, 85, 105
Guyanas 116

Haida tribe 24, 28; carving *21*;
    mask *24-5, 29*; totem *28*; whale
    hunting 24
Halach Uinic 92
He who shoots at the Stars 69
Hiawatha 28
High Priest of the Rains 69
Hopewell and Adena Mound 40
Horse, American 13, 14, 45
House of Flowers 62
House of the Frog *66*
Huari 130, 134
Huascar 152
Huaxtecs 54, 58
Huayna Ccapac 152, 153
Huemac 63
Huitzilopochtli 65, 69, 71, 74, 80;
    birth *68*
Humboldt current 119
Hunting 18, 36, *see also particular
    tribes*
Huron Indians *34*
Inca 8, 41, 84, 93, 117, 127, 130, 142,
    143-54; bridges 147; irrigation
    148; Manco 143; military system
    148-9; pottery *149*; roads 146-7;
    terraces *152*; Topa Yupanqui 150,
    151, 152; walls *153*
Indian: encampment *24*; knife,
    California *15*
Inti 127, 145
Intihuatana *144*
Iroquois 28, 36-8; agriculture 36-7;
    clothing 37-9; defence 36; hunt-
    ing 37
Itzá 95, 96, 105

Jaguar masks 120
Javahé tribe *135*
Jivaro Indians 126

Kalasassaya *130*
Karajá tribe 134, 139
Kashinaua tribe *139*
Katun 100
Kivas 42, 43
Kraho Indian *107, 112*
Kukul 85
Kukulcan *86*, 96

Lacondones 105
Lima 131, 138
Llama 11, 15, 41, 147
Lord Eight Deer Ocelot Claw 51, 67,
    68
Lord Eight Deer of Tilantongo 51
Lord: of the Breath of Life 63; of the
    Market Place 70; of Tilantongo
    67; of Tollan 62
Los Danzantes *46*, 50
Lucayans 114
Lyoobaa 51

Machu Picchu *133, 144*
Macuilxochitl *68*

Magellan Straits 15, 41
Maize 18, 19, 33, *34*, 35, 36, 42, 45,
    63, 73, 74, 85, 89, 112, 115, 117,
    122, 147
Maku Indians *113, 138*
Mama Ocllo 143
Mandans *37*, 79; burial ground
    36-7
Man Friday 114
Maracaibo 115
Marajo Island 112; pottery *121*
Marquesas Islands 151
Maule river 150-1
Maya 35, 54, 63, 85-108, 109;
    agriculture 89; art *101*, 103-4;
    astronomy 100-1; buildings *88-9,
    90-1, 94*, 105; calendar 89,
    97-103; carving *108*; children 92;
    frescos *98*; hunting 89; language 105;
    mythology 101; picture writing 86;
    pottery *102, 104, 104*; sculpture *87,
    92, 93, 104*; Stele K *87*; Stele P *88*;
    technology 103-4; theatre 92-3;
    vase *56-7, 102*; warfare 91-2; women
    92; writing 50, 86, *88*
Mayapan 96
Medicine Man *37*
Metates 43
Mexico 8, 11, 14, 19, 33, 35, 41,
    45-63, 65, 66, 69, 78, 79, 82, 84, 85,
    86, 105, 109; art 46-7; City 14,
    54, 67; Great Lake of 65, 74;
    language 46; pottery 46; sculpture
    45; Valley of 54, 62, 63
Mississippi 11, 40; Indian pottery *43*
Mitla *50*, 51
Mixtec Indians 51, 66-8, 81, 84;
    goldwork *53*; manuscripts 67;
    pottery *68*
Mochica 127, 131-5, 138, 142;
    bronzework 131; painting *145*;
    pottery *119, 131*; vases *140-1*
Moctecuzoma II 70-1
Moctecuzomatzin I 69
Moctecuzomatzin Illhuicamina 69
Moctecuzomatzin Xocoyotzin 70-1
Mohegan Indian carving *39*
Monte Alban *49*, 50
Monument Valley *19, 30-1*
Mother Earth *see* Earth Mother
Muisca 116, 117; goldwork *121*;
    pottery *120*; textile *122*

Nauhuatl languages 109
Nasca 122-6, 130; clothing *123*;
    pottery *123, 124, 128, 131*; vase
    141
Natchez 40
Naymlap 135
Neolithic life 28
New Mexico 81
Nicaragua 109
Northwest Coast Indians 21-32;
    art 24; fishing 30; fur trade 21;
    mythology 27; social system 24-5, 30;

tools 28-9; weapons 29; women *32*
Nuiúe 62

Oaxaca 51, 81
Ohio 40
Olmec 47-51, 58, 86; art 50-1;
    buildings 48; carving *49*; culture
    50; pottery 48, 50; writing 50, 51
Ometecuhtli 63, 73
Ona 15
One Ahau 97
Oregon Indians 21
Orinoco 35
Otomí tribe *64*

Pachacamac 134, *154*
Palenque 54, 93
Palma, Totonac *51*
Panama 11, 109, 114, 115, 116, 153
Paraccas 121-2, 125, 127; figurine
    124; mask *125*; textile *129*
Paraccas Cavernas culture 121
Paraguay 109
Paraguayan Chaco Indians 41;
    pottery 41
Paramonga *138, 149*
ᴾarfleche 36
Patagonian giants 17
Pemmican 36
Peru 8, 33, 41, 109, 119-42, 143, 146,
    153, 154; coastal desert *122*
Peten 85, 89, 95
Pictun 100
Pizarro 153, 154
Place of the Four Directions *see*
    Tahuantinsuyu
Plains Indians 14, 36, 40, 79
Plumed serpent *61*
Pochteca 81
Polynesians 29-30
Pomeiock *38*
Popayan art *117*
Potato 35
Pottery 35, 46, *see also particular
    tribes*
Pueblo Indians 41-3, 81; argiculture
    42; organization 43; towns 43, 45;
    women 43
Pyramid of the Moon 54
Pyramid of the Sun 54, *59*, 62

Quauhxicalli 70
Quebec 11
Quechquemitl, Aztec 75
Quechua Indians *137, 145*
Queen Charlotte Islands 24
Quetzal bird 76, 85; feather head-
    dress *53*
Quetzalcoatl 58, 63, 66, 67, 71, 74,
    80, 96
Quetzalcoatl I 62
Quimbaya 116, 117, cannibalism
    117; pottery *120*
Quipus 145
Quito 152; Scyri of 117, 152

Rain God: Aztec 69; Zapotec 51
Raleigh, Sir Walter 116
Recuay pottery *140*
Rhea 18
Rocky Mountains 11, 13

Sacsahuaman *132*
Sapa Inca 145, *150, 151,* 152;
    Huascar 153
Scyri of Quito 117, 152
Sí 142, 149
Sinú 116
Sioux Indian *26*; painting *31*
Spanish 14, 62, 63, 67, 71, 84, 91, 97,
    105, 114, 115, 116, 143, 149, 153,
    154
Stelae 85, 91, 101; K, Maya *87*;
    P, Maya *88*; Tepatlazco *55*
Stone Age 15, 17, 32, 41, 45, 112,
    128, 155
Street of the Dead 54
Sugar cane 112
Sugar maple 37
Sun God 63, 116, 146
Supreme Justice 70
Suya tribe *138*

Tahuantinsuyu 143, 150, 151, 152,
    153
Taino 112-4; carving *114, 115*;
    tools *114*
Tairona 115; goldwork *116*
Tajin, temple 54; pottery *79*
Taumotu Islands 151
Tayasal 96
Tecpan 105
Tehuantepec, Isthmus of 51, 62
Tehuelches 15, *17,* 18, 35; hunting 18
Tejas 42
Temple: of the Inscriptions, Palen-
    que *57*; of the Jaguars *96*; of
    Quetzalcoatl *59*; of the Sorcerers,
    Maya *64*; of the Sun *99,* 149, 154;

of Warriors *60, 97*; of the Wind
    and Rain *59*
Tenochtitlan 69, *74,* 76, 80, 83, 84
Teotihuacan 54-62, *59,* 84, 85, 86;
    art 58; frescoe 62; pottery *63*
Tepaneca 65
Tepexpan 45
Tepexpan man 14, *14*
Texas 42
Tezcatlipoca 63, 65, 74
Tezontli 83
Tiahuanaco 126-31, *130,* 134, 138,
    143; carving *111*; pottery 62,
    128-30
Tierra del Fuego 11, 14, 15
Tikal 89
Tilantongo 67, 68
Titicaca, Lake 127, 130, *132*
Tlaloc 96, *97*
Tlaloc Tlamacazqui 69
Tlatilco pottery *48*
Tlaxcala 84
Tobacco pipes 40, *40, 41*
Tollan 62, 63, 65, 67, 68, 95
Toltec 62-3, 66, 67, 68, 74, 78, 79, 81,
    84, 96, 97, 103
Tonalpouhalli 71
Tonatiuh 80
Topa Inca Yupanqui 150, 151, 152
Topiltzin Quetzalcoatl 63
Totem pole rock *19*
Totemism 25
Totems 21, 25, *25, 28*
Totonacs 54, 58, 86; carving *51*;
    palma 51; pottery *51, 54*; writing
    54
Toxiuhmolpia 72-3
Trickster, the 63
Tsimshian 28
Tula 62, 84
Tukuna tribe *138-9*
Tun 100
Tupí Indians 112, 114; language 109

Tutul Xiuh 96
Two Reed 71-2

Uaxactun 86
Uetlatoani *67,* 69, 70, 76; Ahuitzoltl
    80
United States 11, 19, 28, 33, 41
Uxmal 96, *103,* 105

Vancouver, Captain 21
Venezuela 112, 115
Venus 62, 63, 74
Vera Cruz 47, 48, 54, 63
Viracocha 143, 145, 153
Virginia Indians *36, 38*

Wampum 39
War of Flowers 84
Waura Indians 106
West Indies 71, 109, 114

Xicalanca 58
Xingú river 138
Xipe Toltec 74, *75*
Xiuh 95; clan 96; Tutul 96
Xiuhtecuhtli *67*
Xolotl *71*
Xochicalco 62
Xochipilli *56*

Yaghans 15, *16*
Yahuarhuaccac 143
Yopico 74
Yopis 84
Yucatan 63, 95, 97
Yucatec: culture 96; Maya building
    60-1; towns 95

Zapotec 51, 62, 67, 86, 89; art 51;
    buildings 51; carving *46;* pottery
    51; writing 50, 51
Zuñi pueblos *32*

159